This River
Beneath the Sky

A YEAR ON THE PLATTE

Doreen Pfost

University of Nebraska Press
Lincoln and London

An earlier version of chapter 1 was previously
published in *Platte Valley Review*, Fall 2009.

Library of Congress Cataloging-in-Publication Data
Names: Pfost, Doreen.
Title: This river beneath the sky:
a year on the Platte / Doreen Pfost.
Description: Lincoln: University of Nebraska
Press, 2016. | Includes bibliographical references.
Identifiers: LCCN 2015021583
ISBN 9780803276796 (paperback: alkaline paper)
ISBN 9780803285347 (epub)
ISBN 9780803285354 (mobi)
ISBN 9780803285361 (pdf)
Subjects: LCSH: Natural history—Nebraska—Platte
River Valley. | Landscapes—Nebraska—Platte River
Valley. | Pfost, Doreen—Travel—Nebraska—Platte
River Valley. | Nature observation—Nebraska—Platte
River Valley. | Nature writers—Nebraska—Platte
River Valley—Biography. | Platte River Valley
(Neb.)—Description and travel. | Platte River Valley
(Neb.)—Environmental conditions. | Nature—Effect
of human beings on—Nebraska—Platte River Valley.
| Nature conservation—Nebraska—Platte River
Valley. | BISAC: NATURE / Ecosystems & Habitats
/ Rivers. | NATURE / Animals / Birds. | HISTORY
/ United States / State & Local / Midwest (IA, IL,
IN, KS, MI, MN, MO, ND, NE, OH, SD, WI).
Classification: LCC QH105.N2 P43 2016 |
DDC 508.782—dc23 LC record available
at http://lccn.loc.gov/2015021583

Set in Garamond Premier by L. Auten.
Designed by N. Putens.

For Mark and Andrew

CONTENTS

ACKNOWLEDGMENTS

The story of the Platte River would be incomplete without the stories of people: those who live and work on the river and those who have felt the river do its work on them. I am grateful to the many people who shared their time and stories with me; some of their names appear in the text: Alan Bartels, Kenny Dinan, the late Charles Frith, Karine Gil, Deb Hann, the late Jack and Pat Hann, Carol Hines, Rita Johnson, Steve and Cyndi King, Ron Klataske, Gary Lingle, John Murphy, Ed and Sil Pembleton, and Kirk Schroeder. The recollections of several other people improved my understanding of Platte River conservation efforts. I am indebted to Bessie Frith, Gene Hunt, Marge and Bruce Kennedy, Glennis Nagel, Grant Newbold, Bill Taddicken, and the late Margaret Triplett. Thanks also to Joe Methe, who introduced me to Rita Johnson.

Earlier versions of chapters 1, 3, and 11, plus portions of chapters 2 and 9, were part of my 2008 master's thesis at University of Nebraska–Kearney, where I earned an MA in English with a creative-writing emphasis. I appreciate the guidance I received from my thesis committee: Barbara Emrys, Susanne Bloomfield, and Robert Murphy. In addition, Susanne introduced me to the Western Literature Association, which recognized "Trailing Consequences"—a slightly abridged version of chapter 3—with the 2011 Frederick Manfred Award.

This book begins and ends at the National Audubon Society's Lillian Annette Rowe Sanctuary. I could not have written it without the help and encouragement I received from the staff and my fellow volunteers at Rowe. In particular, Keanna Leonard, Kent Skaggs, and Bill Taddicken have been there since I became a volunteer in 2005, and they have made me feel as if I have a home on the river.

Thanks most of all to my husband, Mark, and to my son Andrew for their understanding and support. This book is for them, with love.

THIS RIVER BENEATH THE SKY

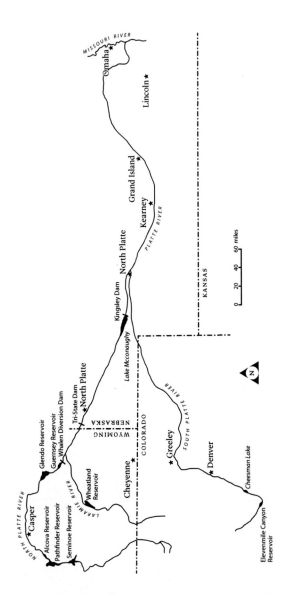

MAP 1. The North Platte and South Platte Rivers originate in the
Rocky Mountains and meet in Nebraska to form the Platte River.
U.S. Department of the Interior/U.S. Geological Survey.

I *Swept Up in a Wind-Borne River*

MARCH AND EARLY APRIL

Their voices arrive first. A distant, soft-edged trill rolls toward the quiet, gray river. Soon, a flock of birds, flying in a lazy V formation, materializes in the southern sky. As it flies closer, as the voices grow louder and sharper, each gray bird becomes distinct, its neck outstretched, legs trailing behind. I raise my binoculars and watch the slow sweep of wings, the upward flick of wingtips. After ten months' absence and a daylong flight, two hundred sandhill cranes are announcing their return to the Platte River. Their voices rise in pitch and intensity as they approach, as if they were elated to be here at last. Or perhaps it is only I who am elated. The flock skims across the channel, toward the north-bank meadow. The V collapses as the birds cup their wings in six-foot arcs that tip, glide, and tip again, while cranes fall like pattering rain.

This is how spring arrives at the Platte — not with the flip of a calendar page, but from little clouds blown in on a southerly wind. The first sprinkles began weeks ago, but by early March every day ends in a steady shower of cranes.

A second bugling flock glides into view, then a third. Then more. And more. Flocks coming in from the south are new arrivals. Others approach from north and west, from cornfields where they have been feeding since morning. They drift down to the meadow, smooth as smoke; just before they drop out of sight behind the streamside brush, the pale undersides of their wings flash golden in the late-afternoon light.

The sun sinks lower in the sky; all around, black tendrils appear to be rising from the horizon, interweaving, drifting nearer, converging on the river. Flocks of Canada geese and white-fronted geese trade back and forth above me, in search of an evening roost. Meanwhile, cranes continue pouring by the hundreds into the north meadow. Now come the snow geese — three hundred, four hundred, a thousand — in a glittering web that unravels across the sky. Bugles, honks, and squeaks blend in a steady, low-level din that washes across the river. Each passing flock sounds like a wind gust that swells to a roar as it approaches and then fades away.

Twisting clouds of cranes begin to rise from the meadow. They swirl for several seconds and fill the air with piercing bugles. The cranes spill down in waves, landing first on sandbars and then wading into the water to make way for those who follow.

A great roar rises downstream, and within moments the sky is churning with dark and white geese, up above, all around, swarming toward the sunset. Above the wading cranes, a fluttering gray and white blizzard of ten thousand geese piles up, hundreds of feet in the air. An invisible floor slides out from under them, and they drop down, filling the river, obscuring the water.

The last sliver of the sun dips below the earth's rim; above it, stacked bands of orange and blue are strewn with black flecks — each fleck a bird, flying toward this river. The flecks stretch on and on, disappearing in the distance. In the thickening darkness, trumpeting, flapping silhouettes rain down onto the river all around the blind. All around one solitary human. Gradually the fluttering storm abates. Minutes pass; the voices grow calm. And finally, we are all still.

Thus is the Platte River valley transformed once a year from a region of cultivated fields and docile livestock into a land that's wild with birds. "Spring" migration actually begins in February, with waterfowl — geese and ducks — arriving from their wintering grounds, primarily in Texas and Mexico and along the Gulf Coast. Individual ducks and geese may stop over on the Platte or in the Rainwater Basin wetlands south of the river, for only a few days each. But as the first birds depart, more and more arrive, swelling their numbers through early March. All told, the waterfowl number in the millions. Meanwhile, the number of sandhill cranes rises throughout March, with individual birds stopping here for three or four weeks. Waterfowl and cranes alike are here for the same reason — this is the place that offers water in which to roost and a bountiful food source on which to fatten up before continuing north to the breeding grounds. In no other place along the Central Flyway can migrating waterbirds find a quantity of habitat that so precisely satisfies their needs. And in no other place on earth can a person sit beside a river and see this many sandhill cranes.

On a spring evening in 1970, a thirty-six-year-old graduate student from Kearney State College hunkered down beside the Platte and took notes as thousands of sandhill cranes flew overhead. Charles Frith was not only a midlife college student; he was a professional wildlife biologist who had put a successful career on hold to go back to college and earn a master's degree — all because he had something important to prove. In his job with the U.S. Fish and Wildlife Service, he was responsible for evaluating the effects of dams and other federal water projects on wildlife and for recommending measures to limit or mitigate any environmental damage resulting from such projects. But in 1967 he was assigned to evaluate the Bureau of Reclamation's newly approved Nebraska Mid-State Reclamation Project, a plan to divert water from the central Platte River during periods of high flow and store it in reservoirs for irrigation use. Within months, he became convinced that the project would devastate the Platte River habitat on which hundreds of thousands of cranes depended. Frith had compared his agency's surprisingly scant data on sandhill cranes with what he had observed in the six years since he had moved to Nebraska. He believed the Fish and Wildlife Service's survey methods had led the agency to significantly underestimate the number of sandhill cranes along the Platte. Just as importantly, he was sure that a failure to understand *how* the cranes used the habitat had led the service and others to dismiss the river's importance to the species. Indeed, some people, observing cranes in the meadows and cornfields, questioned whether the river channel was necessary at all. It appeared in 1967 that no one was going to object to the Mid-State Reclamation Project and its likely effects — unless he did. And if he wanted field data to bolster his argument, he'd have to get them himself.

Based on his experience with the Bureau of Reclamation, Frith may have had little hope of preventing the project: in its heyday, the bureau usually got what it wanted. But perhaps his research could alter the project in a way that would preserve at least some habitat. At the very least, he would go down fighting.

Out in the meadow, Frith watched as a flock of some six

hundred cranes and another of three thousand flew in from opposite directions and converged. Minutes later, a huge flock — he estimated fifteen thousand—rolled toward him and filled the sky. He watched and waited, until it was too dark to see.

Before dawn in mid-March, I lead a group of visitors down a riverside path toward an observation blind. Treading slowly and softly, I listen for the steady crunch of gravel behind me — an indication that we're at a comfortable pace for walking in darkness. Somewhere beside the path, a ring-necked pheasant, startled from his hideout in the grass, squawks and flies off with a resounding whir of wing feathers. We're startled, too: I hear several gasps — including my own — then muffled, embarrassed laughter.

For the past several years, this is how I have spent many mornings in March — as a volunteer guide at the National Audubon Society's Lillian Annette Rowe Sanctuary, one of a few places where visitors can get a close-up view of spring migration on the Platte. In early 2005 I read in the newspaper that the sanctuary needed volunteer naturalists to help greet the thousands of visitors who converge on the Platte each spring. I needed something, too — something to lift me out of the funk I'd been in since moving six months earlier to Kearney, Nebraska, where my husband had a new job. It wasn't Kearney's fault, really, or Nebraska's fault. Mostly it was me, and my longing for the home I'd left behind, so that nothing here pleased me, not the farm fields; not the railroad towns or the open spaces between them; and certainly not the dreary, inconstant river that, as if through lack of initiative, followed the route of the interstate highway.

So, Rowe Sanctuary. In exchange for leading groups on tours and answering questions about the migration, I would see cranes for free, as often as I wanted. It sounded like a fair trade. In Wisconsin and Illinois I had occasionally had the good luck to see two or three dozen sandhill cranes at once; the prospect of seeing a thousand or so at a time sounded like something that would lift my spirits.

With ten other new volunteers, I attended five weeks of Saturday morning training sessions at the sanctuary. We learned about sandhill cranes — their behavior, their natural history, and their reliance on the Platte River. We discussed the logistics of leading a tour group and became familiar with the sanctuary. Then in early March we received our final class: a dress rehearsal of a blind tour, led by a longtime volunteer named Robert. We gathered beneath the front awning at the sanctuary's headquarters, the Iain Nicolson Audubon Center, shortly before sunset. Robert stood off to the side of the group, so we were looking not at him but at the fields where cranes were foraging or at the sky, where they were flying. The first words he spoke were from Paul Johnsgard's book *Crane Music*: "There is a river in the heart of North America that annually gathers together the watery largess of melting Rocky Mountain snowfields."

Within seconds, I fell under the spell of the Platte River. As I listened to Johnsgard's words, snowmelt cascaded down mountainsides in my imagination; floods and broken ice surged through river channels to splinter tender saplings, hurl sand about, and carve new, sudden channels that split and converged, sweeping the whole works toward the Missouri River. Suddenly, I lived in an interesting place.

That night we saw, not a thousand cranes, but ten thousand or more. They streamed toward the river and clouded the horizon. Those of us who had never seen such a sight stood frozen, astonished as hundreds of shouting cranes slipped from the sky, as if on gossamer threads, and landed just a few yards away. Meanwhile, hundreds more swirled and swirled around us, binding us, with those invisible threads, to each other and to themselves. We were part of the cranes that surrounded us, of every crane that had answered the Platte's call for untold thousands of years, and of every crane that would return here in the future. And we were all part of the wild, dancing stream that used to be.

I glance over my shoulder now, and behind my group I can see the sun's glow spreading across the east horizon. We have enough light to see our feet on the ground and the silhouettes of the trees along the path. We reach the old wing dike, where we turn to walk the last few yards to the observation blind. Our view of the river — and more importantly, the cranes' view of us — is blocked by a tall wooden fence, but we can hear. We are walking into a babel of honks, squeaks, and bugles — the voices of thousands of geese and cranes, including many quite near the blind.

I open the door of the blind and step aside to let the group file in. Faces and shapes are barely visible in the shadows; I study them and try to recognize individuals and recall our brief conversations when we gathered at the Nicolson Center. This morning I have, among others, three wildlife biologists from Colorado; an amateur photographer with a load of gear; five men and women from Japan with their local host; a reporter from Wyoming; a woman, also from Wyoming, who impulsively made a reservation yesterday after reading the opening scenes of Robert Powers's novel *The Echo Makers* and drove all night to get here; two couples from New Jersey who are apparently a pair of bird-watching friends and their less enthusiastic wives; a retired couple from Wisconsin; and several bird-watchers from Lincoln who say they come here every year.

Soon, everyone has chosen a window in the L-shaped blind, some facing west and others looking north across the river. Now we wait.

We peer into the darkness at ghostly movements. All these eyes, day after day, staring at the river, looking for cranes. It's strange to think that until a few decades ago almost no one was looking.

I have been reading a 1974 master's thesis that I borrowed from the university library. Its author, wildlife biologist Charles Frith, was the first person to document much of what we now regard as common knowledge about crane habitat on the Platte River. Unlike many graduate students, who struggle to identify a gap in current knowledge as a starting point in their research, Frith had a topic that contained more gaps than knowledge.

It seemed that nobody knew enough to predict whether — or how — sandhill cranes would be affected if more water were removed from the Platte. So Frith set out to study cranes on the Platte — exhaustively. He photographed channels and meadows throughout the year to demonstrate seasonal variations; he studied aerial photos from the National Archives, comparing the conditions of channels in 1938 and 1968; he borrowed a night-vision scope to study movement of birds after dark; he noted the stretches of river where cranes roosted — and where they did not — and waded or recruited friends to help paddle out to measure channel widths and depths; he knelt in the meadows and inspected the vegetation and soils where cranes had been feeding; he interviewed farmers, bird-watchers, hunters, game wardens. He even drove to wildlife refuges in Texas and New Mexico to observe the behavior of sandhill cranes on their wintering grounds.

One of the most significant outcomes of Frith's study was

that he defined the characteristics of sandhill crane habitat on the Platte River: broad, shallow channels with bare sandbars; open areas with views unimpeded by trees or tall vegetation; and adjacent wet meadows.

Almost all the central Platte River was, to varying degrees, degraded by reduced stream flows and consequent encroachment by trees and shrubs. Only three stretches were still in what Frith called "pristine" condition and provided good crane habitat. "Every effort," he wrote, "should be made to preserve these areas." One of those three areas is the stretch of river I'm looking at through the window of the blind at Rowe Sanctuary.

The source of the commotion we have been hearing comes slowly into view as the sun rises. Right outside the blind are thousands of snow geese. Most are pure white but for the tips of a few black wing feathers. They are swimming on the water, jostling about in a space that is confined by a gray-feathered wall of cranes standing a wingspan apart and stretching on for perhaps a hundred yards. Beyond them is another broad white swath of snow geese . . . then gray for as far as I can see.

To our north, several hundred cranes stand on and around the nearest sandbar. While less dramatic than the mass of birds to our west, they are equally captivating because they are so close that we can see their very faces, even without binoculars. Several birds stand tall and alert, their long necks extended as they survey their surroundings. Others begin to walk, with slow, stilted steps. One takes a drink, bending forward to dip its bill horizontally into the river and then stretching its head and neck toward the sky.

The birds' voices blend in a low murmur, punctuated every few seconds by bugles as cranes fly over in twos and threes, heading either for a new spot on the river or for the cornfields.

The geese — more edgy and nervous than cranes — spook at wind gusts, at low-flying birds, at almost anything. With each alarm, patches of a hundred or so yelping birds leap up and flutter briefly, like a tablecloth being shaken out on a windy porch. Then they settle down until the next time. The fluttering keeps us all in suspense, anticipating a big liftoff.

It happens without warning: some signal, perhaps the angle of the sun or something beyond the bounds of human senses, tells ten thousand geese in one instant that it's time to go. With a heart-jolting "boom," a white wave rolls upward around us and crashes against the sky. The throng surges westward and pulls the next swath of white wings upward in its wake. And far upstream even more birds rise, so that within minutes, the western sky is a shimmering silver curtain that hangs in the air for a full minute and then slowly, oh, slowly the curtain thins and evaporates.

I watch the cranes, expecting them to follow. They stir but do not fly. The sun rises higher and spreads a golden-russet light over everything; the grasses on the north bank and the naked trees seem to glow. Even the cranes are lightly gilded. "Oh, look," someone sighs at the sight, and several people raise their cameras.

I walk slowly along the back wall of the blind, watching people. For indeed, I have found that contrary to what I might have expected, I enjoy watching not only the birds but also the humans who delight in the birds. The wildlife biologists look through binoculars at the cranes on the sandbars and occasionally whisper to each other. The woman who drove all night from Wyoming leans against the edge of the window and gazes out; she looks deeply content. One of the women from Japan smiles at me and shakes her head in apparent wonder.

The cranes are more active now and restless. A few make

stiff-legged leaps and then fan their wings upward and bow low, their foreheads near the ground. The leaping and bowing seems contagious, and soon the flock is fairly bubbling. One pair begins a unison call. The male throws his head back, bill pointing straight upward, and bugles repeatedly. His mate responds, with her head tilted not quite so high and with shorter, higher-pitched calls.

A bald eagle, its black wings pumping fast and steady, appears in the east, flying upstream. A low rumble spreads like distant thunder and rolls to a crescendo as the cranes burst into the air, bugling and flapping. Inside the blind, we are all looking up at a scene that is too vast for binoculars. Some people wear broad smiles; others hold their hands over their mouths. The reporter has lowered her camera. The couple from Wisconsin crouch beneath their window. "Unbelievable!" the husband repeats. "Unbelievable!"

Cranes fill the sky; their trumpeting voices echo in our bones — a strange communion with these people I have scarcely met. And although I am with them, I am also utterly alone beneath these swarming heavens.

Small groups of cranes thread the sky as we walk back to the Nicolson Center. A few people speak softly to each other and point out cranes in the cornfield, in the sky. Mostly we walk in silence. I am walking at the back of the group, watching my companions, and thinking of some of the reasons people have given me for traveling hundreds of miles and rising before dawn to come here, often multiple times.

The wildlife biologists are here, perhaps, to recharge their batteries after too many hours in a Denver office. The Wisconsin couple came because they learned about the Platte during a tour of the International Crane Foundation in Baraboo.

Photographers come here for images they can capture nowhere else in the world. Kearney residents seem proud to share a local wonder with out-of-town guests. We have all seen what we came to see . . . but there is something more. Something that leaves many of us feeling strangely at peace, our emotions spent.

Regarding myself, I know the truth. It would be nice to say I wake at three o'clock in the morning and drive here to spread the word about protecting the Platte River and sandhill cranes. But what I'm really after is that rush of adrenaline, the visceral thrill that makes a person exclaim, "Unbelievable!"

As young children in Michigan, my friends and I were wild for playing in summer thunderstorms. We ran from porch to porch, getting drenched, calling for the wind to blow harder, for the thunder to peal louder. We are all grown now and more sensible. But at least one of us still craves that feeling of inundation.

In *The Power of Myth*, a series of interviews filmed for public television in the 1980s, journalist Bill Moyers asked Joseph Campbell whether humans throughout the ages are on a quest to grasp the meaning of life. Campbell, a scholar of mythology and a student of the human spirit, replied, "People say that what we're all seeking is a *meaning* for life. I don't think that's what we're really seeking. I think what we're seeking is an *experience of being alive*." In these moments of pure experience, we forget our little selves and slip out of the skin that walls us off from the rest of the living world. To experience *being alive*, we have to step off the porch into the thunderstorm.

In early April I begin to watch for signs; the cranes will go soon. Their schedule is unforgiving: The birds that travel farthest need more than a month to reach destinations as far away as the Yukon, Alaska, or eastern Siberia. There they'll build a four-foot-wide nest on some marshy ground, incubate a pair of eggs for about a month, and then raise one or two chicks to adult size before snow arrives and fall migration begins in September.

Some instinct helps them strike a balance between storing enough fuel in their bodies and heading north in good time. By now, they are just waiting for the right weather: migrating weather.

On a sunny, almost-warm morning, my husband Mark and I are walking through a sand prairie west of Kearney and two miles from the river when we hear a remotely familiar but hard-to-place sound. Hard to place because we haven't heard it for a year: the call of departing cranes. It is almost the same bugling we've heard each morning on the river but with a faintly different timbre: ever so slightly higher pitched, as if the cranes are calling each other to stick together and hurry up. We search the sky for several seconds before finally spotting the silvery squiggle high overhead: about a dozen birds are setting out for the tundra.

Spring migration is beginning to end. I mentally rearrange my calendar for the next few days: Can I get to the river tomorrow? Tuesday as well? Responsibilities wait at home — my office needs cleaning, the checkbook needs balancing — but all those things will be here after the cranes have gone.

After sunset Mark and I take a walk along the old rail bed to the trestle bridge that spans the south channel. For the first ten minutes of our walk, the river is obscured by trees along the path. But as we approach the bridge, we know cranes are in the water; we hear their voices ruffling on the breeze. I recognize a mixture of feelings that I've had in quite different surroundings — in airports.

In an airport, the person leaving and the person left behind may dread the moment of saying good-bye, but while they wait outside the security gate, they have already begun to separate and to think about what's next in their diverging futures. Meanwhile, outside the terminal, metal birds prepare to migrate, and the ease with which they leap across miles makes all the world seem thrillingly close. Miami, Rome, and Montreal lie just beyond a few doors.

Watching the supple gray creatures rise from the water, circle dreamily, and float back down, I picture the landscape of North America sliding past beneath their wings. A seven-thousand-mile stretch of the continent lives on the map these cranes carry in their minds. North Dakota's Lostwood Lakes are there. Then Saskatchewan, the Northwest Territories, and the Yukon. Places that, to a castaway in Nebraska, seem almost imaginary are suddenly as real and as present as these cranes.

Tomorrow's forecast calls for south winds and sunshine. By midday that sunshine will heat the dark soil in the cornfields. The warmed earth will cook the air just above it to create thermals — rising spirals of air — which the cranes will ride upward, up until they catch a tailwind that carries them north. They haven't left yet, but I can already feel the blank moment that follows a departure, when it's time to think about what's next.

The following day, I am sitting in the kitchen, where the late-morning sun slants across Charles Frith's thesis on the table before me. It does not end on a hopeful note. He predicts that further water development — in this instance, the Mid-State Reclamation Project — will eventually cause the remaining crane habitat to become degraded as stream flows dwindle and channels fill with trees and other plant growth.

"Likewise, the Sandhill Crane resources of this continent will be affected by the changing ecological conditions of a very complex habitat and will experience a yet unknown fate."

Fortunately, a great deal has changed since he wrote those words. While Frith's thesis did not explicitly oppose the reclamation project, local opponents of Mid-State used his research to bolster their argument. Ultimately, the project was defeated by a public vote in 1975. Meanwhile, Frith's efforts had attracted the attention of conservation organizations, most notably the National Audubon Society, which purchased land in one of the three "pristine" reaches Frith had identified.

In 1967 when Congress approved Mid-State, which would have spelled almost-certain destruction of the central Platte River, the fate of sandhill cranes attracted little notice. Today, spring migration attracts tens of thousands of tourists and bird-watchers, and therefore it attracts the attention of local communities, businesses, and chambers of commerce. Kearney, Gibbon, Minden, and other communities regularly host "Crane Watch" events. The Stuhr Museum in Grand Island hosts "Wings over the Platte," which includes an art show and a speaker series. Local and state newspapers and magazines feature front-page photographs and news stories. Jane Goodall comes to town. Secretaries of the interior drop by.

And so the Platte River may benefit from the same principle that protects large flocks of vigilant migrating birds: anything is safer when many eyes are watching.

As I read and take notes, I'm interrupted by voices — glittering threads trailing across the sky. I step onto the front porch and watch a series of flocks, each a loosely shaped V of about two dozen cranes. They are coming from the southwest, from cornfields around Rowe Sanctuary and Fort Kearny. And it might just be my notion, but they seem to veer at the bottom of Linden Drive, to fly right over my house before setting a course due north. No one else is outside. Many of my neighbors are at work somewhere else, at desks or behind counters. I wonder if I am the only person in Kearney who had her window open on this April morning, the only one who recognized that matchless sound, and the only one who right now is looking up.

At Rowe Sanctuary everyone is looking up. I arrive midafternoon, having abandoned the possibility of work, and find a small group of people in the parking lot, all elated, like me, by the warm breeze and sunshine . . . and by the leave-taking flourish in the sky.

Above the river a flock of some thirty cranes are rotating on an invisible axis that tilts first one way and then the other. With each tilt, the spreading gray wings vanish and rematerialize, like a knife blade glimpsed edgewise and then full-on. And like knife blades, the wings flash silver when they catch the sun. Vanish . . . flash . . . vanish . . . flash. We shade our eyes with cupped hands and follow the rising vortex. In an instant, the wheeling mass reshapes itself into a linear wave, its apex pointing at the arctic. The wave rises in the sky beyond the Platte. Each pair of wings slowly shrinks to a speck and is gone. The trumpeting notes of alp horns trail behind. They rise in pitch and echo across the valley.

Another echo rises behind us in the field across the road, where two and now three cranes unfurl their wings and gather up the wind. Some of their companions continue to feed or to laze on the ground. Others look up, shift restlessly, ruffle their feathers. A few stretch their wings. The bugled shouts sound urgent. One bird arcs its neck and takes several quick steps with wings outstretched. Then another bird takes off. And another. Within a few minutes, half the flock is in the air, circling, tilting, rising.

All the while, something within the airborne bodies tugs them north. The circling mass drifts over the road, above us, and then farther north, above the river, where they flash, vanish, and flash in the sun. And circle higher. From hundreds of yards away, voices call from the fields all around, signaling that they, too, are nearly ready.

Part of me yearns for the flock to spiral downward and stay one more day. But much stronger is a feeling of exuberance that soars with the sandhill cranes and looks down on the Platte and then north toward tomorrow, toward the open sky into which these birds will soon vanish one last time.

But not really the last time. In half a year, we'll hear that high-pitched bugle again and look up to see a flock heading south in a glittering, waving line. And shepherded by the birds who leave us today will be new chicks, hatched on the tundra.

Some of the southbound flocks will slow and circle a few times above the river — instruction, perhaps, for the young birds who must memorize their route from arctic barrens across the boreal forests and Great Plains to their wintering grounds and back again the next spring. Back again. As our planet orbits a life-giving, death-giving sun, spinning us each day from darkness into light and back again, the cranes retrace their ancestral course.

Standing in the parking lot, with Platte River sand beneath our feet, we smile and silently bid farewell to the vanishing flecks. The cranes will go north — for now — and those of us who stay behind will keep an eye on the river.

2 *Regarding the Aftermath*

Seeing the Platte right after the cranes' departure is like walking downstairs the morning after a wild party. The revelers are gone, and the absence of their voices — of their energy — seems palpable. Instead of used highball glasses and water rings on the coffee table, they have left footprints on sandbars and a few pale feathers that twirl on the current and race downstream.

For those of us left behind, it's a bit lonely at first, but it's also a relief. I can stay home, sleep late, free of the certainty that I am missing the party's highpoint. When I take a quiet walk, I can just look at the river.

And shiver. It's hard to believe that just a few days ago we unzipped our jackets, tied the sleeves around our waists, and shaded our eyes from the afternoon sun as we watched flocks of cranes flying north. Today, both the sky and the river are dull, steel colored, and roughened by a chill west wind.

Entering the shelter of an observation blind, I button up all but a few windows at the northwest corner and look around at the river itself — easily overlooked when it's full of cranes.

Easily overlooked, even though it is the whole reason the cranes stopped here — the party's dance floor, if you will. Plus the bar and buffet.

The stretch of river that crosses Rowe Sanctuary is managed specifically to replicate the habitat that cranes and other birds once found on the Platte River, and so it provides a glimpse of what the central Platte used to be: a braided stream across an open plain.

Looking down from the window of the blind, I watch multiple currents weave and twine around long, narrow sandbars. The currents alternately blend, swerve, or split in a mosaic of riffles and eddies. Here and there, sandbars merge to form cul-de-sacs where rivulets slow, pool, and sometimes lazily reverse course.

Until the twentieth century, the Platte River was a braided stream that on a typical April morning would, for much of its length, have resembled the scene before me outside the blind. In some ways, though, this river was profoundly different, especially in the way it behaved.

Before the Pawnee relinquished this land to settlers and before the Platte was tamed, its flows varied fantastically over the course of a year, in a way that is commonplace in western streams but almost unimaginable east of the Missouri. Fed by the Rocky Mountains' snowpack as it melted and flowed downhill, the Platte River's two principal tributaries, the North Platte and the South Platte, swelled in late spring. Downstream from their confluence near the present-day city of North Platte, the Platte River in June was often over a mile wide. From mid-June through late summer the flows diminished, and the river might, in years of little rain, dry up completely. In autumn the stream flowed low or moderately, winding around sandbars and islands that emerged as the water levels dropped. Grasses, shrubs, and trees might have a chance to sprout, on some islands and on the banks, before winter.

But at the end of winter the tender sprouts were torn loose and washed downstream in the chaos of ice breakup and flash floods caused by ice dams.

Later, repeating the cycle, June floods finished the work of scouring away plant growth as the sediment-laden river shaped, shifted, and erased sandbars and spread across the floodplain.

A few of the largest islands divided the river into two or three narrower channels; on these bits of land — sheltered from prairie fires and bison — willows, cottonwoods, and forest shrubs eked out a living.

The low banks, similarly scoured and flattened, offered little resistance to the sprawling waters. Thus, the banks, like the sandbars, were mostly bare of trees, except for a widely spaced band of cottonwoods that marked the extent of the active channel. Meanwhile, as the river rose, so did groundwater, which percolated into sloughs and old channel scars, further blurring the line between channel and floodplain. In most places, bankside trees and shrubs succumbed to the combined onslaught of floods, bison, and prairie fires. What grew instead along the banks were lush grasses, sedges, and wildflowers — a ribbon of tallgrass winding through the midst of Nebraska's semiarid mixed-grass prairies.

When pioneers came to this region, they found an erratic river with a quicksand bottom — fit neither to ford nor to float. Settlers found a violent and unreliable stream that washed out their bridges and flooded their homesteads in the spring but ran dry when they needed it to water their crops.

And so it stayed, until settlers and developers set to making the wayward stream an upright member of society.

The first major dam projects on the Platte River system were harbingers of the water demands to come. The Cheeseman Dam and Reservoir, on the South Platte, was completed in 1905; a few years later, it became Denver Water's flagship storage facility. On the North Platte, Pathfinder Dam, completed in 1906, stored about a million acre-feet of water for irrigation in Wyoming and western Nebraska. In subsequent years, additional reservoirs with capacities totaling over four million acre-feet were built on the Platte River's tributaries for irrigation, municipal storage, and — providing revenue to help pay for dam construction — electric generation.

Of course, damming a river does not empty it of water. Local rainfall drains into the Platte as before. Municipal water, after it is used and processed through city treatment plants, comes back to the river. Some portion of irrigation water exceeds what crops take up, and it, too, flows back toward the river. And water released from hydroelectric generation flows right back to the channel. But a great deal of water — including what is lost to evaporation — never returns to the Platte.

By the year 2000, researchers estimated that annual flows in the river had diminished by half. But there is not simply less water. There is less of almost everything that made the Platte River what it was, beginning with the natural cycle of floods and low flows. Today, the amount of water flowing in the central Platte usually depends more on the gate operators who release reservoir water than on the seasons, the weather, or the snowpack in the mountains.

Deprived of its force — and also of its sediment, which remains trapped behind the dams — the river is less able to build, shift, and scour sandbars. The loss of sediment leads to incising — meaning that the water cuts down into its own bed. Thus, the "mile-wide" river of legend in many stretches grows narrower and deeper, less likely to flood the wet meadows along its banks.

But there are fewer wet meadows, in any case. Many have been drained and converted to crop fields. Others, in the absence of prairie fires, have been overrun by trees and brush, as have the river's banks and much of the channel itself. Of trees and other vegetation, the Platte River has not less but much, much more. Where high flows once swept away any plants before they achieved a year's growth, trees have taken root and grown to maturity, turning portions of the once-active channel into riparian forest. In most stretches, water flows between fringes of tall, thirsty invasive weeds: purple loosestrife and phragmites, or common reed grass. Even here at the sanctuary . . .

"*Nee-nee-neep*."

A lone shorebird flies past the blind and lands at the edge of the nearest sandbar. The greater yellowlegs, about a foot tall, is a gray-streaked bird with a long, thin bill. Its large, dark eyes, surrounded by a white ring, give it a rather soulful look. It scampers along with its head down and dips its bill into the shallow water to detect the motion of minnows and invertebrates on which it feeds. For the greater yellowlegs — as for sandhill cranes, whooping cranes, and most waterfowl — south-central Nebraska is migration habitat. Although the birds are absent from this region for most of the year, the habitat here plays a crucial role in their lives. It enables them to survive the rigors of spring migration and reach their breeding grounds in good condition and ready to nest and perpetuate their species.

I watch the yellowlegs tottering along on the sandbar and think, "It could have been worse." Although vast stretches of the Platte River are badly degraded, the Platte valley and the Rainwater Basin wetlands to the south still fuel the spring migration not only of the yellowlegs and other shorebirds but of a half million cranes and several million geese and ducks. Water pulled from the channel produces the corn on which they feed. And in places where people have cleared away trees and weeds, the channels and wetlands still provide a secure evening roost.

It could have been much worse. In the 1970s, '80s, and '90s, the central Platte was just a few bad decisions away from destruction. As Colorado, Wyoming, and Nebraska continued a dispute older than statehood over who had the right to how much water, a variety of agencies and organizations proposed water development projects for a variety of purposes: surface irrigation, groundwater recharge, flow reregulation, flood control, electric generation, power-plant cooling, municipal needs, possible *future* municipal needs.

Any of these projects might have been enough to tip the scales and reduce the stream flow so drastically that the remaining channels would dry up and become overrun by trees. Conservation organizations, both public and private, banded together to defeat most projects, through legal action, lobbying, and grassroots campaigns. In addition to protecting the river, some organizations also began habitat restorations on thousands of acres, so that today, despite the trees and the many weed-choked channels, cranes and waterfowl can generally find a stretch of open river like this one every few miles. In addition, some restored channels contain specially constructed islands that provide nesting habitat for two other species that rely on the Platte — least terns and piping plovers.

But habitat restoration and maintenance are costly — in terms of both money and labor.

Continued work depends largely on a combination of federal

and state funds and private donations to nonprofit organizations, all of which are subject to the vagaries of the economy.

Since 2008 an important prospect for stability in Platte River habitat work has come from the Platte River Recovery Implementation Program (PRRIP). PRRIP is a pact between the states of Nebraska, Colorado, and Wyoming and the U.S. Department of the Interior that curbs water use and pools resources for funding habitat protection and restoration along the central Platte. One of the program's goals is to improve the timing of stream flows to help maintain in-channel habitat. If it succeeds, more and more stretches of the Platte may eventually look like the stretch at Rowe Sanctuary. But the recovery program is a plan, not a guarantee. The states' governors signed it with the understanding that any of the states may withdraw at any time, for any reason. At which point, the program would cease.

With or without the program, the Platte River, like any other water source in the Great Plains, has a future filled with uncertainties, especially in the face of climate change. Climate scientists predict that a combination of higher temperatures and less precipitation in the Rocky Mountains will reduce annual snowpacks — meaning less water may flow into the Platte system's reservoirs.

Meanwhile, higher temperatures will increase evaporation, both from reservoirs and from crop fields, further reducing the supply of irrigation water, while at the same time increasing the need for it on farm fields. A conflict like that might lead irrigators in one state or another to call for withdrawal from the recovery program. Furthermore, worsening habitat conditions on the wintering grounds of many bird species will increase their dependence on food sources along their migration route.

In conservation, a pact, project, or legal victory is never the end of the story; it's just the end of a chapter . . . and sometimes not even that.

"*Nee-nee-neep.*" The greater yellowlegs takes flight and, with a flash of white tail feathers, heads upstream. In a week or two, it will be on its way north to breeding grounds in Canada. As water becomes more scarce in the Great Plains, we are almost certain to hear voices that question whether we can afford to squander so much water for birds that are seldom even here, when Denver needs more water to keep growing, corn crops need more water to keep growing, and power plants need more water because *everything* keeps growing and needing more electricity.

An upright member of society must juggle many responsibilities, and the Platte River is apparently no exception. Time will tell if the recovery program can balance the needs of agriculture, cities, and wildlife, too. Still, it seems only fair that, even as it fulfills its many obligations, the mostly tamed Platte River should be allowed to kick up its heels for a couple of months each year and throw a really fine party.

3   *Trails and Consequences*

MAY

In 1879 a twenty-nine-year-old writer from Scotland rode the train west across the United States. By the time he crossed the Missouri River, he'd been ill for much of the journey, and San Francisco was still several days away. There, he hoped to join the woman he loved — who was still married to another man.

Robert Louis Stevenson had enough to distract him on his cross-country trip, yet he stationed himself atop a fruit wagon and looked around as he crossed the prairie. He later wrote, "We were at sea — there is no other adequate expression — on the plains of Nebraska."

When Stevenson crossed the Great Plains, the transcontinental railroad was already a decade old, and Nebraska had been open to settlement for a quarter century. So there were homes and budding communities here and there along the way, but it was the space between those homes and communities that affected the young man. "It was a world almost without feature," he wrote, "an empty sky, an empty earth; front and back, the line of railway stretched from horizon to horizon, like a cue across a billiard-board; on either hand, the green plain ran till it touched the skirts of heaven." It was the sort of view that could make a person feel like an insignificant jot on the landscape, as people often seem to feel when standing before mountains or an ocean — or beneath a sky full of cranes. But that was not how Stevenson felt. Instead, he wrote, it seemed to him that the train had become huge in the vast expanse. "Even my own body or my own head seemed a great thing in that emptiness. I note the feeling the more readily as it is the contrary of what I have read of in the experience of others."

It may be fruitless to speculate why Stevenson felt like a "great thing" in a circumstance that made others feel small. He might have had some idiosyncratic way of seeing the world, or his perceptions might have been skewed by his malaise. If I put myself in his place, though, I imagine that on a treeless plain I might have a primal feeling of vulnerability, like a prey animal with no place to hide. Perhaps such a sense of being unsheltered and exposed is like feeling unnaturally large. Paradoxically, then, it would not be so different from "feeling small."

Fruitless to guess, but I think about it anyway as I walk beside the Platte, where the dense trees ensure that I will not feel unsheltered. From the sanctuary's bluebird trail, where I walk in early May, there are no views wide enough to remind me that I am, indeed, an insignificant jot. I do feel large — ungainly even — but for a reason unconnected to empty land and sky.

I hold nest box number 9 in my hands, and in it is a nest with four just-hatched bluebirds. Their naked, purple-pink bodies are no bigger than a fingertip and so fragile looking, it seems that even my gaze might bruise them.

Number 9 is one of thirty nest boxes I impulsively agreed to watch over one morning during my first spring in Nebraska.

The cranes had been gone for a week or so, and I must have looked in need of something to do, because when I bumped into the sanctuary's director, Paul Tebbel, after a walk by the river, he asked, "Do you want a project?"

Though I had never monitored a bluebird trail before, I'd heard of them and knew their purpose. Populations of bluebirds, which nest in the cavities of trees, had spiraled downward in the middle of the twentieth century. They were threatened in part by human tidiness: in parks, yards, and woodlots, we tend to clear away the dead and dying trees where bluebirds might find nest holes. But a greater threat came from two ruffian species — house sparrows and starlings — that competed for the spaces that remained. Both house sparrows and starlings are nonnative birds, brought to eastern North America by humans in the nineteenth century.

The aggressive foreign birds spread westward across the continent and might have entirely crowded out many native species if not for a group of bluebird devotees who founded the North American Bluebird Society. The national organization, through regional affiliates, distributes nest boxes designed to be easily installed, monitored, and kept clean and safe by human helpers. Not only bluebirds benefit. Tree swallows and house wrens also find homes on Rowe Sanctuary's bluebird trail.

I could have asked Paul if he thought mid-Nebraska had been part of the eastern bluebird's historic range. Uncharacteristically, though, I didn't much care. What I cared about was being needed.

If no one *needed* me to walk the sanctuary trails each week, I probably wouldn't go. Too many other things needed doing, even though what *I* needed was to be outdoors on a regular schedule. At first I could not articulate that need, but I recognized it later in Stevenson's critique of the Great Plains and his image of a settler benumbed by a monotonous landscape: "Our consciousness, by which we live, is itself but the creature of variety. Upon what food does it subsist in such a land? . . . A sky full of stars is the most varied spectacle that he can hope for. He may walk five miles and see nothing; ten, and it is as though he had not moved."

While Stevenson's criticism sounds harsh, it's true that to a newcomer's eyes, not much varies on the Great Plains from one mile to the next. But from one week — or even one day — to the next, there is variety enough to nourish a starving consciousness.

I gently return the cylindrical nest box and its tender cargo to the steel post that suspends it five feet above the ground. After scribbling "4 BB — 1 day" on my chart, I head to the next birdhouse, looking around at changes that have occurred here since my last walk. Trees that were bare when April ended are tipped with green; in the sandy soil beside the path, early blossoms of spiderwort — purple, three-petaled flowers the size of nickels — nestle between long, tubelike leaves; and new grass has sprouted through last year's thatch.

But most of the changes that occupy me on the bluebird trail revolve around the growth of tiny birds. Last week, the tidy cup-shaped nest in box number 9 held four turquoise eggs, perfect as pearls in a jewelry box. In the next two or three weeks, barring calamities — high winds, hail, torrential rain, ninety-degree heat, and hungry predators are all typical of Nebraska spring — the young birds will grow from wiggling, fuzz-covered nubbins to fully feathered little birds that will blink gravely at me when I peek into their nest.

That is in the future, though. Today I have one bluebird nest with eggs and three others with young. At box number 14 the adult birds perch on the barbed wire fence a few yards off while I check their brood. They'll wait until I have walked away and then resume the job of parents the world over — keeping the family fed. Seldom is that job performed with such grace as the bluebird unintentionally achieves. In a sudden blue flutter, the bird springs from its perch, hovers like an idea for just an instant and then swoops to snatch an insect in midflight. With another flutter, the bluebird regains its equilibrium and then delivers its catch to an eager yellow bill that's waiting within the nest.

Box 15, the last one on the trail, has been claimed by a pair of tree swallows. The female flies out when I pull the nail that holds the door in place; the male sits on the fence. The door swings down, and there is the swallows' nest, a cup at the bottom quite like a bluebird's but lined with soft white feathers curling upward in a delicate arch, like the boudoir of a fairy princess. I reach out to part the feathers with my fingers and see how many eggs . . . *whoosh*. A winged missile shoots past my head — low. As I snap the door shut and fumble with the nail, I try to look up without raising my face to my tormentors. Here are two swallows whose reproductive effort will go unrecorded this summer. I hunch my shoulders and stride away — they'll not have the satisfaction of seeing me run — and duck my head as they dive and snap, snap, snap their fierce little bills.

By the time the swallows are through with me, I have walked to the top of a sandy ridge that runs parallel to the river. The ridge is part of a narrow strip of sand-dune habitat — a microcosm of the Sandhills to our north — that formed on the Platte's south bank millennia ago from windblown sand. The rest of the region, outside the riverbed, is blanketed by richly fertile loess, or "glacial flour," a dust-fine soil that blew in when glaciers covered eastern Nebraska. Even Robert Louis Stevenson might acknowledge the variety on this sand ridge, dotted with prickly pear cactus, amid land that once was a soggy tallgrass prairie.

Something rustles near my feet, and I look down just in time to see a long, slim lizard's tail flicker and vanish in the grass. Racerunners favor these sandy spots where vegetation is sparse and they can shoot across the bare ground like tiny arrows. The lizard's neon-green head and back are eye-catching; the male also has a bright blue underside, from its face to its belly. Faint stripes extend from the racerunner's back to its tail, which makes up more than half its length. But I have seldom glimpsed these details for more than a few seconds before that brownish tail slips down a bank or into a clump of shrubs. Just once I would like to dive after one and hold it in my hand for a closer look. My field guide offers a worthy excuse for not trying: "Racerunners are well named, usually winning the race with the would-be collector." But the truth is I have another reason for shrugging my shoulders and saying, *Maybe next time*. I've heard that they bite. It might be an exaggeration to say I'm afraid of a lizard that weighs little more than a first-class letter. Even if one bites my finger, he won't bite it off. Still, if ever I should try to catch one, the half-second hesitation in which I think of those tiny teeth will probably cost me the race.

After walking within a quarter mile of the Platte for nearly an hour, I have yet to see the river, but I am constantly aware of its presence. Were it not for the ribbon of water that winds across the plain, there would be no ribbon of trees in this semiarid climate. And I would see few of the birds that surround me today.

Just before taking a path through the trees — toward the river at last — I hear a turkey gobble some fifty yards back on the bluebird trail. Through binoculars, I can see that he's fanned his tail and puffed his body feathers into a shape as round as the make-believe birds on paper napkins at Thanksgiving. Even if he did not do such a fine imitation, though, a real bird is better than any idealized one, and for many years Nebraskans had little or no chance of seeing a real turkey in the wild. By the early twentieth century, this state — like many parts of the country — had lost its last turkeys to hungry settlers and market hunters. In the 1950s and '60s, however, Nebraska wildlife biologists transplanted turkeys from other states and regulated their hunting. Since then, the population has flourished, and I seldom fail to see a few turkeys, or even a large flock, while walking near the river.

The turkey on the bluebird path, strutting and gobbling for some females that must be nearby, is a reminder that May is courtship season on the Platte. While bluebirds and tree swallows are already in the throes of parenthood, many other birds at the sanctuary today are still choosing — or trying to attract — prospective mates.

The crane migration provides one type of spectacle on the Platte; the month of May provides a more varied display, as all types of birds — migrants and residents — put on a show for each other, singing and dancing. We are not the intended audience, but that can't reduce the pleasure of watching.

The brown-headed cowbird is so bold you'd think I *was* his audience. Perched on a low, exposed branch beside the trail, he arches his wings umbrella-like, drops his head, and puffs his feathers, singing all the while. The cowbird sounds as if he took the same voice lessons as his cousin the red-winged blackbird, but the duller bird got a C- on his report card. His song is wheezy and lacks the redwing's resonance. The cowbird's voice need not carry far, though; for he does not sing to stake out his territory. Cowbirds have no nest territory, because they have no nest. Instead, the female lays her eggs in the nests of other birds, often removing or even destroying one or more of the "legitimate" eggs. Some encroached-on species recognize the cowbirds' eggs as stowaways and toss them overboard. Other hapless songbirds, though, incubate, hatch, and feed their larger step-children while their own young, outmuscled at feeding time, starve.

The cowbird's approach to parenthood sounds corrupt, but for a nomadic bird that once roved the prairie, feeding among grasses cropped short by wandering bison herds, foster care was simply a practical survival tool for both parents and offspring. Their impact on victimized species was as widely dispersed as the wandering bison.

But now cowbirds feed instead among cattle, whose movements are hemmed in by barbed wire. Likewise, the warblers and sparrows that nest near forest edges are hemmed in by corn fields, highways, and housing developments. So the cowbirds' parasitism, instead of being an occasional nuisance to one bird or another, can become a threat to the survival of entire species that have limited nesting ranges.

On his perch, calling for a mate, the brown-headed cowbird knows none of this. Nor is he aware that I am admiring his fine looks — the glossy iridescence of his feathers, the graceful arc of his wings — beauty that humans might judge to be at odds with his base reputation. But cowbirds are guilty only of being cowbirds. They survive in the way that cowbirds always have, and we are their accomplices.

In the bottomland, where trees and shrubs have been growing and dropping leaves for many years, the soil is rich, muddy in places, and pocked with deer tracks that point the marshy way to the water's edge. As the ground begins to ooze beneath my feet, the river comes into view — at last — and a little song twirls about in three-quarter time: "*waltz* with me, *waltz* with me, *waltz* with me." The common yellowthroat, its come-on notwithstanding, is secretive and shy; so even when I know one is nearby, I don't always bother to look for it. Today, though, I am with a yellowthroat who refuses to be overlooked. So I pause for a while to watch the tiny olive-colored warbler dressed for a costume ball, in a black eye mask, flitting from one dogwood twig to the next. His nest is bound to be nearby and might soon harbor cowbird eggs. In any case, he'll keep singing all summer, and we might meet again when I take this path to the river.

From my spot beneath the branches, I see two river channels, maybe a third, streaked with low, flat sandbars. Beyond these channels is a long, steep-banked green island, two feet above the water's surface and thickly covered with grasses and sunflowers. This was a sandbar that lost its identity. One summer, perhaps a decade ago, a few plants sprouted on the bare sand when the water was low. At first it looked like green fuzz. But by fall some of those plants had sent down roots deeper into the sand, so that when the water began to flow again in September or October, roots held the sand in place. Months later, the spring floodwaters — a fraction of what they had been before the river was tamed — had too little power to swamp the sandbar and uproot the plants. Instead, the sand piled up around the roots, and the strip of sand became a stable island, now dozens of yards long.

Beyond the island, there might be a trickle of a channel among the weeds, and then beyond that is a tangle of trees and shrubs not quite as dense as the one where I stand. I squint and try to see a mile-wide river . . . to no avail.

I follow the path toward my car and nest boxes 1 and 2, which I skipped before. A pair of house wrens are settling into box number 1, the male having first stuffed it with dry twigs to impress his lady. She'll finish the nest now, carrying bits of grass for a soft lining. They chatter and scramble about, their flight and song both like a looping roller coaster, first on my left and then my right. Their energy and volume seem incongruous in a half-ounce package with plain-brown-wrapper plumage. One of the pair perches on the box and scolds me; they'll be even noisier next week when I open their roof to check for eggs.

Above the treetops, wild chatters and buzzes interrupt the wren, and I lift my head to see two eastern kingbirds spiral upward in a feathery helix. They tumble-pivot-plunge and then climb again. Both birds fan their black-and-white tail feathers as a magician fans a deck of cards.

The courtship rituals of wild creatures — and arguably of humans — are demonstrations of fitness, of a prospective mate's ability to produce and provide for healthy offspring, who in their turn will reproduce and perpetuate their parents' genes. It makes sense, then, that eastern kingbirds, which earn their living by snatching insects in midair, would show off their flight skills during courtship. What matters to me, an outsider standing on the ground, is that they are beautiful. Perhaps it matters to them as well. If in nature beauty is the equivalent of that which is good and fruitful, then perhaps the kingbirds have some awareness of each other's beauty.

I watch them fly off together and once again thank Paul for giving me a project. Without it, I might have finished more work at home today, but I might also have gone all my life without seeing the courtship dance of the eastern kingbird.

Often, when standing at the water's edge, I try to imagine a different Platte River — the one that flowed between the lines of covered wagons, the one that astonished and vexed nineteenth-century emigrants and adventurers. At this time of year — when the bulk of wagon trains passed this way — the river would have been on the rise and may have spanned a mile near the bluebird trail.

Francis Parkman, a young historian from New England, rode the trail west in 1846, not as an emigrant or adventurer, but as a researcher on his way to meet and interview Plains Indians. Parkman described the moment when his party, on horseback, crested a hill and first surveyed the Platte. The river valley, he wrote, "had not one picturesque or beautiful feature." The river itself held no appeal for him either, although his description is somehow appealing to me: "For league after league, a plain as level as a lake was outspread beneath us; here and there the Platte, divided into a dozen thread-like sluices, was traversing it, and an occasional clump of wood, rising in the midst like a shadowy island, relieved the monotony of the waste."

Parkman recorded what he saw because of his profession, but many amateur diarists on the Oregon and Mormon Trails also wrote about their experiences. Historian Merrill J. Mattes spent decades poring over more than seven hundred of these first-hand accounts and compiled them in *The Great Platte River Road*, an encyclopedic summary of the westward migration.

Mattes estimates that 350,000 emigrants traveled the Council Bluffs Road, or Mormon Trail, on the river's north side and the Oregon Trail on the south between 1841 and 1866. Although wagon trains crossed the Missouri River at various points, the Platte valley was where all paths converged, because it formed a natural boulevard with a gradual approach to the Rockies.

Even to travelers less critical than Parkman, the Platte was a strange-looking creature that, according to Mattes, gave some observers the impression that it flowed above the level of the land. He quotes Martha Missouri Moore, a newlywed traveling west in 1859: "The river is a perfect curiosity, it is so very different from any of our streams that it is hard to realize that a river should be running so near the top of the ground without any timber, and no bank at all." Earlier emigrants than Moore recorded that while the banks were treeless, the larger islands held timber; however, by Moore's time, those trees might have been felled as construction material for Fort Kearny, built in 1848.

Parkman, Moore, and others who followed the Little Blue River along the Independence–St. Joe Road crested a hill near the present county line between Kearney and Adams Counties, about ten miles south of Shelton. It is still possible to follow the approximate path of their approach and to stand at roughly the same spot from which most emigrants first saw the Platte.

The sweeping view of the river valley from that spot is even now a stirring sight: rain-carved loess hills that surround Denman Avenue roll down to a flat lowland stretching east and west to the horizon. Far to the north, the loess hills rise again, looking like a rumpled blanket. Except for topography, though, little remains of the curious landscape that amazed the emigrants.

If an overland migrant landed on the crest of that hill today, she would see tractors lumbering across the valley and the metal skeletons of center-pivot systems to irrigate corn and soybeans where the prairie grasses grew.

Each square-mile section of land is portioned off by roads that form a relentless grid; here and there, fences and windbreak tree lines further fragment the once-unmarked plains.

On hills unsuited for a plow, cattle graze in the place of bison, whose tremendous herds must have seemed inexhaustible. William H. Kilgore, who traveled on the north side of the Platte in 1850, recorded an encounter with a herd: "I see more Buffalo this afternoon than I had any Idea of Seeing on the whole trip. They extend the whole length of our afternoons travel and they are not in hurds but in Solid falanx." The following day his party passed another herd: "I am not able to [make] anything like a Satisfactorial estimate, but I have no hesitation in saying I Saw two millions." The animals Parkman saw on the south side of the river were more scattered but still fantastically numerous: "The face of the country was dotted far and wide with countless hundreds of buffalo . . . and far off, the pale blue swells in the extreme distance were dotted with innumerable specks."

Gone as well are the Pawnees, whose lives were intertwined with those of the bison and who dwelt on and hunted these lands for hundreds of years.

The river itself is invisible, not only lost among a corridor of trees, but reduced to a shadow of what the emigrants saw. If I walked the whole length of the central Platte in the month of May, in no place would I find an expanse of water greater than one hundred yards.

Three hours west of here, in hills above the North Platte River, Ash Hollow State Historical Park shelters remnants of the ruts left by emigrants' wagon wheels. The ruts that started as faint gouges have eroded over the years to become deep ravines in which a person could walk and be shaded from the sun. As inexorably as rain turned those cart tracks to canyons, change trailed the emigrants as they continued westward. And most of the changes far outlasted the trail of furniture and belongings tossed from wagons to lighten their load.

The communities emigrants built — in Oregon, California, Utah — spurred another change, named Union Pacific. Ahead of the approaching rail line, Nebraska became a territory open to city builders and settlers, who planted trees and crops and who found ways to suppress the great fires that were anathema to farms and essential to prairie ecosystems.

Bison, whose enormous herds were a threat to trains, were all but extirpated. The Plains Indians who resisted the iron road met a similar fate.

Within a few decades, farmers began to experiment with irrigation canals and then with dams that gathered the river's flowing water in the spring and held it for the summer growing season.

It's not hard to imagine that a century and a half ago a man or woman who stood on the rim of the Platte River valley would have felt the type of awe that modern tourists seek to experience in mountains or oceanfront vistas. They might have felt, as Stevenson did, "at sea." And like tourists on mountains or cliffs, they might have felt small and insignificant. But when I look around at what humans have done — even humans who were just passing through — I can't help feeling much *too* significant. It's a disturbing power that can transform a landscape and alter the lives of entire populations — of bluebirds and turkeys, cowbirds and bison, and even members of our own species.

From the trail's descent into the Platte valley, it was about a day's travel to Fort Kearny, one of several military posts built to guard the Oregon Trail. Although the fort's main purpose was not the provisioning of emigrants, many did take advantage of the chance to replenish supplies, shoe horses, see a doctor, or post a letter back home.

Travelers camped outside the fort, and Merrill Mattes recounts the practice of arranging a party's wagons into a corral within which livestock grazed on the lush grasses of the wet meadows that lined the Platte. Campfires, fueled mostly with dry buffalo droppings, burned outside the corral, the better to illuminate any approaching perils. Women and children sometimes slept within the wagons, but these were often so cramped that families slept under the stars instead or, when it rained, beneath the wagons.

The original buildings of the old fort are gone now, abandoned and dismantled after the railroad made the overland trails obsolete. In their place is a state park with replica structures and signs to help tourists envision what existed at building sites outlined on the ground.

Much harder to envision is the steady stream of wagons, rumbling between the fort and the river, and hundreds of people camping, preparing meals, and building fires where mile-long rows of corn now grow.

A few miles east of the old fort, I take a sunset walk at the end of May. My trail is the old rail bed where once the Burlington Northern crossed the river to meet the Union Pacific line. Before the railroad, emigrants sometimes waded the channels here in search of a few sticks of island-grown firewood.

Dusk is the time for music. The birds' colors are swallowed in shadows, and their voices rise like myth from the trees. The cardinal's throaty "*sweet, sweet*" gurgles from deep within the cedars, a catbird mews, and someplace a killdeer is shouting "*k-dee, k-dee.*"

A strange clicking sound, like an insect, reverberates insistently among the bottomland trees. I peer toward the sound and make out a — something — a dark mass that must be a bird, but it's such a strange shape, like a fat blue jay. Suddenly the strange shape flutters to a branch just a few feet away and becomes a screech owl, who appears to be as interested in studying me as I am in studying back. Despite its size—little more than a hand span from tip to tail—the owl has a disarmingly fierce expression: a dark V between its round yellow eyes gives the appearance of a frown. The lines of the frown sweep up toward what some people might call horns or ear tufts; to me the owl appears to be wearing a plumed helmet, like a tiny Roman warrior. Looking into my eyes, it speaks in a language that's foreign to me, in a descending interval: "*dee-oo, dee-oo.*" Then it flies quite near my head, clicking its bill again and landing across the trail in a tree whose branches arch over the path. I duck slightly, though I'm mostly just surprised it's so close, not really frightened. "*Dee-oo, dee-oo,*" it repeats, swooping again; I suspect that means "get lost" because the owl's nest is in the cavity of an old tree nearby.

Or rather than shooing me, perhaps the owl thinks to lure me away. In either case, I decide to continue my walk and to stop causing a disturbance, but it leads me down the path, flying back and forth before me as I walk: *click, click, click,* SWOOP, *dee-oo.* I wonder if a bird feels afraid when it defends its nest or if it is quite heedless of risk. This one is small enough that I could stuff it in my pocket, but still it persists. I hunch my shoulders slightly and quicken my pace—SWOOP—until finally, when I reach the trestle bridge, the tiny owl apparently decides it has succeeded and flies away into the shadows.

At the bridge, I emerge into a darkly glittering world. The full moon silvers the flowing water. I look up at the scattered stars, visible despite the glow of Kearney's lights beyond the tree line.

Looking down at the shining river, I try to imagine this much water times five. Then I try to imagine crossing it in a wagon with my family and all that I own. A few emigrants crossed near here — mostly north-route travelers who needed to reach the fort and some south-trail emigrants who thought their chances of escaping cholera were better on the north side.

I like to imagine that I would have been courageous enough to ford this river or that I would have felt only wonder — not panic — at the emptiness of the prairies or the sight of ten thousand buffalo. But it's hard to be sure of my mettle when I'm cowed by tiny lizards and small persistent birds.

On the island between the south and middle channels, a turkey gobbles; I amble over to investigate.

At the island, no shining moon glow reflects beneath the bridge — just darkness, where grasses and cattails cover the low standing water. I hear something else now, not a turkey, but a soft clucking and the muffled *smack-smack* of a hundred little kisses. It's a soothing sound, like a grandmother might make, perhaps, as she rocks an infant to sleep. I could climb down the steps and try to find the singing frogs, but my footsteps would likely startle them into silence. I prefer to stay here and listen.

I think of the overland travelers lying on the ground at night. They must have felt quite small and unarmored after a day beneath the endless sky, perhaps a day of watching bison herds and dreading a stampede. Some must have lain awake, knowing that beyond the circle of the campfire, wolves and other four-legged creatures were prowling. And there were mysterious, dark-skinned people who actually lived on this lonely land. And there was the land itself that rolled on and on, so much of it between here and home — the home forsaken and the home that was still just a dream.

Wouldn't they have longed for a sheltering circle of trees or something that felt like walls or at least like an embrace? A shelter like that might be enough to relieve the despair of being an insignificant jot — or the despair of being all too significant. I sink down to sit on the bridge, lean my head back against a rail. I should go home. I have my own bed to sleep in, beneath a roof, and a family that's wondering where I am. But it's easy to sit still, to think of almost nothing, wrapped in the circle of the frogs' tender voices.

4　*Rooted in Sand*

JUNE

When my brother Carl and I were small, we owned a yellow plastic sandbox shaped like a rowboat. Kneeling across from each other at the stern and bow, we fashioned walled cities and fortresses in the sand. Defense, which every sand edifice needs, required a moat. And a moat required a garden hose.

There are two ways to fill a sandbox moat with water. The direct method is simply to place the hose end in the moat and call for your brother to turn on the tap. If the water flows too quickly, though, the hose leaps from its channel, and water rips through a fortress wall. Even a gentle flow gnaws at the sides of the moat, washes the sand about, and cuts new channels. The moat fills quickly. But as soon as the tap is turned off, the water soaks away.

Call for more water and repeat the process. Eventually the sandbox becomes saturated, and water stays in the moat, but not before erosion takes its toll on the kingdom.

The second method is by insinuation. Dig a little well in the bow of the boat and pour the water in very, very slowly. Too fast, and the well floods. But pour slowly, patiently, just refilling the well each time its contents seep away, and gradually water percolates through all the tiny gaps between grains of sand, spreading to the gunwales and stern of the sandbox. From the surrounding sand, the rising water seeps into the moat and fills it.

Until nature has its say. We ruled the sandbox but not the elements. Our water levels rose and fell with rain and evaporation — forces that also topple sand fortresses. Undiscouraged, we'd kneel in our accustomed places and begin again.

A gravel truck rumbles down the dirt road, and I glance over my shoulder at the billowing dust in its wake. The driver, if he looked this way at all, might have registered a lone woman wading through knee-high grass in a flat, empty field. Maybe he wondered why anyone would take a walk in a place with so little to see.

The truck's clatter has scarcely faded when a glittering, jingling song tumbles across the meadow. I look up at the small black form of a bird hovering ten feet in the air. The bobolink sings and flutters, then sings again as he stiffens his wings into an arc. He glides, drops lower, and the moment he reaches the level of my gaze, ceases to be a plain, black bird. His white back and sunny yellow skullcap flash just before he dives and vanishes in the grass.

I keep walking. It's true that, seen from the road at forty miles an hour, the Platte River's wet meadows in early June look flat and empty. Boring, even. Perhaps I've projected my own thoughts onto the truck driver. Some days I have parked by the road, looked across this meadow, and wondered if I should bother to leave the car. On the other hand, it's also true that the pleasures of a Platte River meadow are easier to feel and hear than to see. As if reading my thoughts, another bobolink starts to sing. I look around and see nothing at first. Then I spot him gliding toward the fence row on my right, where he perches on the topmost twig of an old Russian olive, fifty feet above the ground.

On my first visit to this meadow several years ago, I dubbed it "the Bobolink Trail" in my field notes. The name stuck, not because there was any trail at all — I'm just wandering in grass — and not because I found mostly bobolinks here, but because on my first walk I saw more bobolinks in an hour than I had previously seen in my life. Bird voices mingle in the morning air: meadowlarks, red-winged blackbirds, grasshopper sparrows, and mourning doves. The dickcissels seem to be singing from all points in an endless refrain: "*twiddle-ip, cheep cheep*." Killdeer. Common yellowthroat. Grassland and wetland voices blend. From the shrubs along the fence line on my right come voices of other birds: orchard orioles, brown thrashers, a yellow warbler. The bobolink's song, though, is the one that always makes me pause and reflect on where I am.

This is an in-between place — part land and part river. In between — like the twilight state between waking and sleep, where memories, dreams, and reality flow and mingle. The ground beneath my boots is neither solid nor soft. It seems to give slightly with each step, not because of the deep sand bed that underlies everything for miles around, but because of grass. Last year's grass, gray and dead, lies under this year's fresh green shoots. Beneath the new green and the old gray is a rich layer of soil formed by years and years of old grass lying down, decaying, preparing a place for the new. Though my feet are dry and the river's main channel is out of view beyond a quarter mile of cornfield, I am, as German settlers used to say, "in the Platte." Before me and behind me the ground dips and rolls in a series of parallel swales — graven echoes of the river's west-to-east course.

Even after the Platte settled into its present course more than twenty-five thousand years ago, carving a lazy S shape across southern Nebraska, the channels shifted back and forth, trailing gravel and sand and carving more footprints year after year. For thousands of years, as sun-warmed snow melted and streamed down the Rocky Mountains' slopes, the North and South Platte Rivers swelled and churned through the land that we now call Wyoming and Colorado to converge in present-day Nebraska.

Sweeping southeast from their confluence to the arc of the Big Bend, the waters flooded broad, shallow channels in a miles-wide valley, inundating sandbars and small islands, winding around larger islands, slowing here and rushing there. Where channels curved, water on the outside of the curve sped up and chewed away the sand that blocked its way. Where a current slowed, it began to drop the sediment it had swept up earlier, first gravel and then lighter-weight sand. Under the prairie grasses, sedges, and rushes, the meadows that bordered the shifting streams were made of the same sand and gravel that the Platte had dropped along all its countless paths. The porous ground beneath the Platte's meadows wallowed in the spring with snowmelt and rain, even before the river began its annual rise. As the Platte's surface water rose in May and June, it began to seep and merge with the groundwater, until the water table welled up in the old channel footprints like water filling a sandbox moat. Ground-water mingled with surface water in sliver-shaped wetlands, or sloughs, where chorus frogs trilled and killdeer swooped and cried. And in the early spring, migrating sandhill cranes probed the soggy soil for grubs, mollusks, and other wetland fare.

Although this meadow is mostly dry these days, something ancestral within the cranes must remember when it was a wetland. Wet meadows are a twilight place for sandhill cranes, who feed by day in crop fields. As darkness gathers across the Platte valley, the cranes gather as well, in meadows like this one. They fly in, wave after wave, and feed here . . . until the dark river calls. Then they rise up in great, rippling masses for the short, noisy, stunning flight to the channel.

By the time the cranes flew north in April, this field was scattered with thousands of their gray feathers. Not tufts of down, but ten-inch flight feathers, sturdy enough to dip in an inkwell and write a story. Two months later the feathers have blown away. The corn crop has been in the ground for three weeks and, in most fields, is knee-high, as is the meadow grass around me.

At the edge of a swale, I kneel for a closer look. No water, and the change in ground level is slight — it dips a few inches, perhaps. But that doesn't make the depression invisible. Swales and temporary wetlands are easy to find by their color: even from a distance, the young green grasses seem tinged with rust. Up close, other plants besides grass appear. The brownish-red tips of spikerush, scouring rush, and sedges all bespeak what the eye cannot see — underground water. Wherever the ground dips, the water table lies closer to the surface. It's not as wet as it used to be, but this is still a wet meadow, an island of tallgrass prairie where the songs of grassland birds recall an earlier time.

I turn around, my back to the river that's still a hundred yards away, and sit facing the field I just crossed.

Drawn by a high-pitched "*tik-tik-tik*," I raise my binoculars and scan the barbed-wire fence that marks the cornfield's south border. Two dickcissels perch on the top wire, side by side. Both have golden breasts and golden eyebrows on their gray-and-white faces. But the male's markings are brighter and more distinct, and a black V marks his throat. The female holds shreds of dry grass in her bill — material for a nest that she will build.

The insect-like trill of grasshopper sparrows, "*tsp-chrrrrr*," rises from beneath the grass in several places. An upland sandpiper flutters overhead, announcing its presence with weird wolf whistles. It lands on a fence post a quarter mile away, holding its wings straight up for a moment and then folding them up — fold, fold, fold — like a fancy dinner napkin.

"*Zweep, zweep, zweep*." That's the meadowlark perched on a wellhead, looking out over his territory. Other meadowlarks call from farther away, their voices alternating with the slow coos of mourning doves.

Barn swallows zip back and forth across the grass tops. From a distance, their flight looks as smooth as a shuttle across a loom, even though they are snapping up insects in midflight. Their nests are not in the meadow grasses but in a barn or maybe a shed, probably on the farmstead across the road.

As their name suggests, barn swallows would be as likely to fly over a farmyard or alfalfa field as a tallgrass meadow. Not so for many of the grassland birds that are singing here this morning.

Grassland birds need grass. They need wide expanses of grasses and wildflowers, all hopping and buzzing with insects on which to feed their young. Most build a nest on the ground, sheltered beneath a vault of tall grass. They want an open space without trees — trees that might harbor a hawk or a family of egg-eating raccoons.

I stretch my legs out before me on the ground and imagine what it would be like to wake in this meadow each morning in late spring to the bobolink's song. To lie in bed, eyes closed, and hear, not cars or a train or the neighbor's barking dog, but a jumble of bright notes spilling through the open window. The idea is not so far-fetched. Over by the road, two clusters of cottonwood trees, a quarter mile apart, mark the sites of two abandoned farmsteads — places where somebody once lived.

Old homesites and farmsteads are a common sight on the Great Plains, if you know what to look for: A dozen or so clustered trees all about the same age, with no natural water source to explain their presence. A collapsing barn, an empty foundation. Perhaps a heap of bricks or twisted metal.

There are as many stories, perhaps, as there are abandoned homesteads. Probably more, because people like me make up stories about sites that look interesting. I can make up a plausible story about this meadow just by reading what is written on the landscape. The first thing I read is the ground beneath the sedges and grass: irregular dips and rolls tell me that this is a native meadow, never plowed. If it had been plowed for crops, the man behind the plow would first have leveled the lowest spots; the shallower swales, surrounded by newly erodible soil, would have gradually filled in with silt.

The man who never plowed this land lived in a simple house amid one of the cottonwood stands. He and his neighbor shared the work of building both of their houses. Let's say they were brothers.

These were not first-generation homesteaders — the trees are tall but not thick enough to be a century old. I'll say the brothers were born in a sod house on a homestead thirty miles from here, where their father and oldest brother were still eking out a living on land that seldom got enough rain. The brothers rode their horses around the county every Sunday after church; one day, they crossed the north channel on a newly built bridge and found a lush green meadow quite unlike their home place — and ideal for grazing cattle.

So they bought a quarter section each, built their little houses, and planted their little trees. In an even greater gesture of hope, they married. Maybe they both chose homesteaders' daughters who knew how to milk cows and feed chickens. Or maybe one brother fell for a city girl. Either way, the young brides would have a lifetime of hard work. Maybe they would have been driven half mad by the rattling calls of cranes day in and day out each spring. The grasshoppers in the fall. The howling winds in the winter. But in June, perhaps, there was some consolation in the bubbling song of the bobolinks.

Which brother moved away first? I'll say the one on the east, Brother One, was the first to decide that 160 acres of pasture was not enough to provide for his family. He moved to town and sold his stake to Brother Two, who stayed behind.

The bobolinks paid no mind. It changed nothing if the cattle in the meadow belonged to one farmer or two.

But far to the west, the Platte was changing, and on rivers, change flows downstream. The changes began long before the brothers planted their cottonwoods, sometime in the late nineteenth century when a farmer in the Panhandle, or maybe Colorado, dug his shovel into the ground and, hoping to provide for his family, experimented with digging a furrow to carry the Platte's water to his crops.

Daring men stood in the rain shadow of the Rocky Mountains and envisioned the cities they could build; ranchers and farmers saw how their families could prosper — if only they could harness all that late-spring floodwater and save it for the dry months of July and August, when it would be of some use.

By the midtwentieth century, with six major reservoirs on the North Platte River, plus smaller reservoirs and diversions throughout the Platte system, not only did less water flow through the river, but just as importantly, or perhaps more so, the nature and timing of the flows were altered. Floodwaters that had once poured down the river and percolated through this meadow in June remained instead behind a dam. When the water levels in the channel dropped below the meadow's water table, it was like our sandbox when the moat was dry — the water seeped out of the meadow, not into it.

The meadow was still moist and fertile enough to graze cattle, but one dry summer, Brother Two's neighbor to the west realized that his once-soggy pasture was nearly dry enough to grow a good crop of corn. So the neighbor dug a ditch to ensure the field was drained, and he leveled out the swales so he could cross them with his tractor. Then he broke the sod in the field that I am facing, where corn is sprouting today.

The neighbor had to keep Brother Two's cattle out of his corn, so he strung up a barbed-wire fence, which lies there still, twisted and rusting under the Russian olives, dogwoods, and wild plum that grow in a line. The mixed-species fencerow is the inadvertent work of birds that perched along the wires over the years and excreted the seeds of whatever fruit or berry they had eaten.

Brother Two never plowed this meadow, just kept his cattle on it, even after he and his wife bought a house and moved to town. But upstream and downstream along the Big Bend, more and more pastures became cornfields. Land that had once seemed unsuited to row crops became productive and profitable.

In the 1970s, long after trespassers had carried away the lumber from the brothers' abandoned farmhouses, Brother Two was ready to retire. His sons had moved away — to Denver, Chicago, some place like that — and cared nothing about raising cattle; so when a conservation organization offered to buy the land, he said yes.

I picture Brother Two on a distant April evening, standing on the front stoop of his house to watch a wave of gray birds glide toward his pasture, their calls rattling against the sky. Maybe he remembered those evenings and wanted to keep the place as it had been through all the springtimes when he had watched cranes and all the summers when he woke to the bobolink's song.

Today, conservation organizations own many of the native or restored wet meadows along the central Platte or hold conservation easements that protect the lands from development. A growing number of individual landowners — seeing that cranes and other birds frequent stretches of the river that contain wet meadows — have agreed to restore meadows on their own land as well.

On the way back to the road and my parked car, I walk beside the fence row. The dogwoods, just beginning to bloom, are flecked with tiny white buds. Russian olives, towering and gnarled, are half-dead from old age and half-covered with the showy leaves that look two-toned on windy days.

A brown thrasher flutters out of a dogwood, lights briefly on the ground and then flutters back into the leaves. Most of the songbirds stay hidden in the shrubs, but I can hear who's there: a yellow warbler sings, "*sweet, sweet*," and a mourning dove sighs, "*oo-ah, hoo, hoo*." The orchard oriole stammers out a many-syllable song like his Baltimore cousin's but buzzier. A robin inquires, "*chrrr-up?*" These are the sounds of nature's trade-off. As shrubs and trees grow, new songs arrive in the meadow. But a tree's job is to grow and reproduce. Too much of that, and the bobolink's song would fade from the Platte valley. The upland sandpiper's whistle would still ring through the Sandhills up north, but not here.

The milkweeds are beginning to flower. I leave the fencerow to examine one in full bloom. The flower head, four inches across, is a cluster of dusty-pink flowers shaped like puffed-up stars. The thick leaves, some as long as my hand span, feel like they're covered in fleece. Prairie dogbane, too, are on the verge of blooming. Each flower head is a tiny white bouquet of waxy, pinhead-sized blossoms. Sprinkled here and there, as if they had fallen from the sky, are tiny golden-yellow star flowers.

The breeze carries another sign of June. The teardrop-shaped seedpods of the Platte's innumerable cottonwood trees burst open this month, sending their seed-bearing white fluff across the meadow and down the river with every breeze.

At my feet I find a last reminder of an earlier season. I pick up a feather, white and fluffy at the base, the rest smooth and gray, darker at the tip. The leading edge looks slightly rusty — stained with minerals from the soil with which the sandhill crane preened in a far-off wetland last summer. I slide my finger along the feather's length to smooth its barbs back together. I twirl it briefly, then lay it back in the grass. The cranes never completely leave Nebraska. I suppose none of us ever completely leaves a place where we have been.

Back in town, sitting at my desk, I think of the many home-steaders whose stories survive, and I wonder how many stories have been lost. Settlers whose land stayed in the family remain a daily presence in the lives of their descendants who work the land today. Their great-grandchildren remember and understand the stories of days behind a plow in searing heat, of despair over the torments that dropped from the sky: tornadoes, hail, grasshoppers. They remember their forebears' hope and are the fulfillment of that hope.

For other settlers, those who sold, failed, or perished, sometimes all that remains is a stand of old cottonwood trees and, perhaps, beneath them a collapsed barn, a foundation, bricks, or twisted metal.

The story of homesteader Fritz Langman and his wife Margarethe survives, not through a family farm, but in family stories. Their great-grandson Jack Hann, now in his eighties, keeps a digital family history on his computer. With a narrative addressed to his daughter and son, the history is an open-ended project with photographs and scanned documents reaching back to homesteaders on nearly every branch of the family tree. Jack is following the tradition of his great-aunt Caroline Langman Converse, who wrote several books about Nebraska frontier life, including a memoir called *I Remember Papa*. Converse explains in the book's foreword that she wrote it for Fritz Langman's descendants, so that they would remember her father and be able, in a sense, to know him.

Fritz was a runaway orphan from Germany who worked his way across the United States, first laboring in a Pennsylvania mine and eventually reaching Nebraska. He worked on the railroad at Grand Island and in his free time rode his pony in the countryside, looking for a place to stake a claim. South of Grand Island, near Nine Bridge Road, he found a fertile-looking piece of land covered with lush grass between two river channels. He filed his homestead claim, built a house and a barn, and planted crops on his farm in the Platte. Riding home from a trip to town one day, he stopped at a homestead to ask for a drink of water for himself and his pony. Young Margarethe Rief was on the front stoop churning butter. Margarethe was, in her daughter's recollection, "a plump little body with a round chubby face, pink cheeks and sparkling brown eyes."

Fritz and Margarethe courted and married in July 1874. They had three children — Fred, Caroline (nicknamed Lena), and Arthur. And they had a prospering little farm in the Platte, with a kitchen garden, chickens in the yard, crops in the field, and a faithful farmhand named Hans. Margarethe's sister Anna lived right across the channel, and Fritz grazed his cattle in Anna's pasture. Sometimes a mere trickle separated the properties. But in the spring the water was too high to cross, so Fritz rigged up a ferryboat by caulking an old wagon box and attaching it to a pulley. Margarethe and the children could haul themselves across whenever they wanted to pay Anna a visit.

Things seemed just about perfect for the young family, but Margarethe had one worry: she didn't trust the Platte. Lena's earliest memories were of her mother fretting, "Too close to the river. We're too close to the river."

On Decoration Day in 1883 Margarethe's fears proved well-founded. The melted snowpack from the Rockies was pouring eastward, swelling the Platte into a churning, angry flood. The river overflowed its banks and began to creep across the farmyard. Margarethe, bent on summoning help, herded the children to a dry spot of high land and then waded toward the little ferry, stepped in, and began to haul on the pulley rope. On the far bank, Hans motioned wildly for Margarethe to stay back. She was nearly across the rushing water when the rope snapped, plunging Margarethe and the wagon box into the torrent where they quickly vanished, as her stricken children watched.

Nearly a month later, in late June, a body was found near

Columbus at the confluence of the Platte and Elkhorn Rivers. After a brutal trip down the river, only one thing identified the remains: an engraved wedding ring that read, "Fritz to Margarethe."

I had known Fritz and Margarethe's great-great-granddaughter Deb Hann for nearly three years without knowing of her family's connection to the Platte River. We bumped into each other one November day at a luncheon hosted by the Crane Trust a few miles west of Nine Bridge Road. The luncheon was the trust's way of thanking people who had monitored the just-ended whooping crane migration. I didn't know Deb well; to me, she was the Rowe Sanctuary volunteer who operated the "crane cam" each spring. That involves watching a monitor and moving a joystick ever so slowly to make a remote camera pan the river so that people can watch cranes on their computers at home. The thrill is lost on me, but for Deb it's a work of creativity, choosing where to point the camera and for how long. She gets to see cranes up close and watch the deer that regularly wade across the river among the birds.

At lunch we talked about the latest news from Rowe, about the whooping cranes we hadn't seen, and about my research. Then Deb dropped a small bombshell: "My great-great-grandmother drowned in the Platte."

I gulped. "Really?"

"Yeah . . ." she answered softly.

What does one say about a 125-year-old tragedy? "I'm sorry"? "Do tell"? I missed my opening and said nothing. We ate our lunch.

Later, we took a walk to the riverbank near the trust's offices. Deb told me that as a youngster she had spent countless hours in the Platte. Not just beside it, but in the water. Her mother had packed picnics, and the family had spent entire days at the river south of Grand Island or at a favorite fishing spot near Chapman. "I'd spend the whole day in the river," she said. "When it was deep enough, I'd sit in the stream and bob off the bottom." Deb's mom and grandma set up lawn chairs in the shallow water and let the Platte cool their feet while they watched Deb and her brother play. It occurred to me that I had never waded in the Platte; the realization startled me so much that I said it aloud. "Never?" Deb asked, with a playful twinkle in her eye. "How 'bout now?" We shucked our footwear, rolled up our pants, and splashed in, gasping at the cold and yipping like children one-tenth our age. The river was as clear as the ice water we'd drunk at lunch. And sandy, not gooey like rivers I had waded in Wisconsin. Along the edges of sandbars, the sand was flecked with fine gravel, golden and pink. Pink like our feet. We didn't last long. Dashing from the water, I scarcely took time to brush off the sand before jamming my feet into my socks and shoes, which squished as we trotted, laughing, toward our cars.

Months later, getting dressed one morning, I pulled a pair of clean socks from the back of my drawer and watched sand sprinkle to the floor as I unfolded them. Where'd that come from? Remembering the dropped thread of our conservation, I sent Deb an email and suggested another walk.

We met by the river in late June. The water was low, low enough that we could hopscotch over rivulets and through the weeds from one sandbar to the next. Along the way, Deb told me that her earliest memories included riding out to her father's duck blind in a small boat piled high with decoys and hunting gear. Jack, in chest waders, pulled the boat across the channels, sometimes through floating ice, to his blind on a sandbar. While they waited for the sun to rise over the river, he made breakfast and coffee on a propane stove, and hot chocolate for Deb. At other times of year, they fished together. Whatever they brought home — ducks, fish — was fare for the table.

"Dad taught me to respect the river and nature," Deb said. "He showed me where to look for the deeper and faster spots and how to be safe in the water." She talked about camping in a tent beside the river on family fishing weekends and about wading a mile upstream to reach sandpits where the water was deep enough for swimming.

Deb grew up, moved east, got married, and after thirteen years, returned to the Platte River — alone and seeking solace. She rented a small house between two channels, with asparagus growing in the yard. She bought chickens and goats. "I tried to live off the land," she said with a sigh. "I had lots of eggs and milk . . . and asparagus. But when it came time to kill the animals, I couldn't do it."

I could believe that, since Deb seemed to take heartfelt delight in every creature we encountered — the *cheep-cheep*ing mead-owlark that flew overhead, the killdeer racing about on the sandbars, the tiny young toads hopping in a damp channel bed, even the flowering mullein that I dismissed as an exotic weed. Deb touched a velvety leaf. "I like it," she said in a voice that to me implied, "I approve of all living things."

I was keeping an eye out for one living thing in particular and was soon rewarded with the sight of a fast-flying bird that fluttered like a silvery-white ribbon. I knew that least terns had been nesting on the recently built islands, and here was evidence — the tern flew to the point of a flat-topped island in midchannel and landed near a second bird. Taking off again, it swept past us and along the channel. As delicately as the breeze, it swooped repeatedly, dipping its bill in the water. Finally, it dipped more deeply and emerged with a minnow in its bill, which it delivered to its mate.

We watched through binoculars but kept our distance. Some things are too precious to pursue.

At the end of our walk, Deb suggested that we get together sometime with her parents in Grand Island. We could take a drive to see Fritz Langman's homesite. I headed back to Kearney, planning to search for a rare, old book.

In addition to an account of her mother's death, Lena Converse's *I Remember Papa* tells the story of a man who fashioned a life out of dreams, sweat, and a bit of fertile land. Converse describes not only the rigors of pioneer life but also the pleasures of life in and around the fledgling town of Grand Island, where the family lived in the years right after Margarethe died. There were shows at the Opera House and concerts at the Liederkranz, which the society ladies attended in silks, boas, and long gloves. The local Plattdeutsche Club held picnics, dances, and parades, and the little immigrant community celebrated their new country's Independence Day with fireworks and more parades.

Even when she lived in town, the Platte River was part of Lena's life. The family sometimes made a day of picking wild grapes or buffalo berries that grew in the Platte around Nine Bridge Road.

And Lena spent weekends with her cousin Nellie on her uncle Henry's farm beside the Platte. One of the cousins' favorite recreations was to sneak to the river at night — although it was forbidden — and splash in the water beneath the moon. "We danced and hopped and jumped and skipped about, sandbank to sandbank . . . Sometimes we found a little pool deep enough to sit in."

In a sense, it seems strange that young Lena frolicked in the river that took her mother's life. But the stranger thing would have been for her to avoid the Platte. The river grounded Fritz Langman's family and his descendants in the center of the country where he had earned a home, and it was woven inextricably through all their lives.

A few months later, I met Deb and her parents, Jack and Pat, at a restaurant near Nine Bridge Road, where the three of them were wedged into a booth. I squeezed in as well. Pat looked small and delicate, with a soft face ringed by white curls. Gentle as a powder puff. But when she smiled and her eyes danced like Deb's, I saw the woman who'd caught fish, cooked them on a campfire, and sat on a lawn chair with her bare feet in the river. Jack was lean, all angles and planes, with a hawk-like nose and a serious gaze. I was briefly intimidated and wondered if we would have anything to talk about, but in front of Jack on the table was a stack of books — local histories and Lena's work. Within seconds of our introduction, we were talking about Hall County's early settlers, including so many of the Hanns' homesteading ancestors that I lost count. We talked about changes along the Platte, the proliferation of trees and No Trespassing signs, and the interstate highway that amputated the northern segment of Nine Bridge Road.

In Deb's car, Jack gave directions: "This is the turn here," he said, at a dirt road with a Dead End sign. Then he lifted his gaze to look out across Mormon Island's restored wet meadow. The dirt road became a pair of tracks and then ended at a cattle gate, where a sign told us we were looking at private property belonging to the Crane Trust. "Right over there," he said, pointing south. Nothing. I knew the buildings would be gone; Lena's book said Fritz had moved the brick structures to another farm. The cabin, I assumed, would long ago have lost its battle with the elements. But I thought there might be some sign of a foundation. Maybe a few shrubs. One or two of the cottonwoods Fritz had planted around the farmstead. Nothing. Only a rippling expanse of grass. Fritz's homesite had been between two river channels. We had driven across the north channel, but the stream on the south was little more than a memory. The land dipped, marking where water once flowed. Where I saw a restored meadow and a dry river channel, I guessed that Jack could see much more.

After leaving the homestead site, we drove along what's left of Nine Bridge Road. Jack and Pat tried to name off the locations of the nine bridges. One is north of I-80; at least one was removed from the path of the interstate . . . The remaining road starts from a stub end with a view of the interstate's eastbound lane and a litter-strewn, flooded field — once a wet meadow. From there, Nine Bridge Road doglegs its way southeast across a series of bridge-spanned trickles, a few marshy spots, and one still-broad channel; past a dusty cattle feedlot; and into the village of Doniphan. As we drove north again on Nine Bridge Road, Jack looked around at the ragtag landscape. "This used to be a beautiful drive," he said. "We'd come out here on Sundays just to drive around." I tried to picture a shade-dappled lane with bridges across nine sparkling channels, with families and sweethearts driving along enjoying the scenery. If not for the name on the road sign, I would have guessed we were someplace else.

We drove for hours, bumping down dirt roads, crossing the

interstate, rolling down highways. Jack pointed out landmarks that were invisible to me: the Hann homestead site; the Seiers' homestead, now home to a garden store; the empty foundation of a great-uncle's farmhouse, now hard by I-80; the point of land in the south channel where the Hann men kept a duck blind for many years. The former hay meadow that town kids used to run across on their way to jump into the river is now a city well field, off limits to running kids. At one farm, we studied the bare-wood remains of an old house that had lost its front porch. Jack figured the missing porch was the one on which Margarethe had been churning butter when Fritz stopped to ask for a drink of water six generations ago.

This was the closest I could come to seeing the past, but Jack and Pat could see it all around us, just beneath the surface of blacktopped roads, retail stores, and fences marked with No Trespassing signs. And it seemed to me that as long as they could see it, the lost past was not so lost.

Later, I drove by myself to the Grand Island cemetery and in one of the back-most rows found the big headstone that said "Langman." It was made of red granite and embedded with photographs of Fritz and Margarethe, the same photos that appeared in Lena's book. A wreath had been recently placed on the grave. Strange that this man and woman I had never met, who were no kin to me, stirred feelings as I studied their faces, while the hundreds of other names on the hundreds of other headstones were, to me, only names.

Such is the power of a story that was not only recorded but treasured and retold. In time, Deb may take over her father's job of keeping the stories alive. Or perhaps that is what she is already doing, whenever she leads a friend, barefoot, splashing into the Platte.

Summer solstice. Too often when I take a walk, a small but insistent voice pesters me with reminders that I should be home by a certain time — to get something from the freezer for supper, phone the insurance company, or finally dust the miniblinds. Whatever. There's always something. Today, I have decided not to care about those things. It's nine o'clock in the morning, and I am going to roam around the Fort Kearny trail for as long as I feel like it. I get out of the car, lean against the door, and listen to the world. The cottonwood leaves rustle in the wind. Beneath one massive cottonwood, a bluebird hovers and then dives to snap up an insect.

I begin to walk in a direction I never took before, past a few campers' tents, toward the old borrow pit that was converted into a swimming hole with a sand beach.

I hear a plaintive cheeping and wander around looking for its source. Usually when I take a walk, I carry a pocket-sized notebook to record which birds are singing or what flowers are in bloom. Today I reach reflexively for my notebook and begin to catalogue the items I find on the beach: "three soda cans, three plastic water bottles, one beer can, a cardboard cigarette pack (empty), one pair of flip-flops, an air mattress (partially deflated), a green T-shirt, two disposable diapers (apparently used; I choose not to inspect), a pair of sweat socks, one additional sock, and a park bench, pulled up from its moorings. There are no people in sight, which tells me these things have been here at least over-night, possibly longer. Who lives this way? The mind rebels. I can imagine the lives of Brother One and Brother Two trying to carve out a life on a wet-meadow farm or Fritz Langman riding his pony down the Nine Bridge Road and finding his homestead site. What I cannot imagine are the feelings of people who are content to swim amid their own garbage and waste.

Discouraged, I briefly consider going home, but somewhere a little bird is still calling, *peep! peep! peep!* It is impossible to ignore. I turn away from the beach and toward the thinly scattered trees, following the sound, scanning the branches. *Peep! peep!* Look lower. Right in front of me, almost at eye level, is a hole in a dead, ten-foot-tall trunk. And in the hole is the little brown head of a young flicker, calling for its mother or, more precisely, for its next meal. It seems like a dismal place for a nest, close to a noisy, filthy beach. But the sandy ridge is probably teeming with ants. Like most parents, the flickers presumably weighed the neighborhood's advantages and disadvantages and did their best to choose a place that would keep the family fed. I thrash my way through a patch of shrubs — a shortcut to avoid the beach — and return to the river path.

The sun is a silver-hot disk burning through the veil of clouds. The trees along the path are alive with birdsong: brown thrasher, house wren, towhee. I jot down their names in my notebook and add an asterisk, which means I have heard but not seen them.

Below the bridge, a red-winged blackbird sings in the cattails. Killdeer race to and fro on a stretch of bare sand. But I am looking instead at the great blue heron flying downstream, away from me, with great sweeps of its long wings. Perhaps I startled it. I watch until the wings are just two black curves, ink marks on a page.

I take the stairs down from the bridge to the riverbed below — a tangle of sand and weeds between two feeble channels.

Beneath the weeds, the sand feels powder fine and soft, like a Pensacola beach. In all but the highest places, it also feels saturated, as if the tide had just gone out. The killdeer's tiny tracks intersect chaotically, and here are some larger tracks — long as my hand. The half-dozen tracks end abruptly; on the final track, the middle toe left a deeper imprint. This is where the heron pushed off and became airborne.

Wandering in the general direction of the trickle on the island's north side, I try at first to pick my way around stagnant, algae-covered puddles, until I remember I'm wearing rubber boots and can splash wherever I please.

At the island's north edge, the channel is an elongated Rorschach blot — thin and thick lines of flowing water interspersed with standing pools, some rusty brown, others coated with pale green. The fast rivulet at my feet, though, flows as clear as tap water. I pause and squat to watch sand grains and tiny pebbles tumble along the bottom. Is it my imagination, or can I really hear a faint tick-tick of pebbles bumping each other? I kneel on all fours and lean my head down until my ear is just above the water's surface. *Tick, tick.* It's true.

I stick my fingers into the water, wondering if I can feel the pebbles and sand colliding against me and against each other. I can, but I also feel something that interests me even more. I hold my palm flat, fingertips just touching the bottom. As the water rushes against my fingers and palm and around the back, a tiny storm of sand swirls behind my hand, and sand is swept away from beneath my fingertips, so that I must lower my hand to keep touching the bottom. Behind my fingers, a pile of sand begins to accumulate . . . A sandbar! I try it again. And again.

Deb told me her father had taught her to "read" the river. This must have been one of his lessons. Where there's a snag or an obstruction, the sand piles up behind, but watch out for the deep spot in front.

The sun is getting warmer, and the water in this spot is so clear I am nearly tempted to take a drink. But the memory of wading through muck and the thought of irrigation runoff and municipal wastewater dissuade me.

It was not always like this. As a young man, Jack Hann used to wade out to his duck blind on a sandbar and scoop out a well that filled with water. He drank it straight or heated it for coffee.

It was not always like this. I look up at the bank across the channel to rows of corn, now more than half my height. I keep looking, conjuring trees on that island and men cutting them down to build Fort Kearny. South of the river, I see bison grazing in tall grass that ripples like a river for miles around. The river itself swells in an early summer flood, flattening cottonwood saplings and demolishing wooden bridges. In a farmhouse downstream, a homesteader's son opens a window and hears the bobolink's morning song. And farther east, a young Jack Hann drives down a tree-dappled lane and slips his arm around Pat's shoulder.

I look down at a black squiggle in the clear water. It's an annelid — a water worm — flat sided, like a three-inch eel. Without thinking, I dip my hand back into the water and try to scoop it up. For an instant, it's in my hand; then it slips through my fingers.

My knees, which have not knelt in a sandbox for many years, begin to ache. I stand and walk toward the bridge. Up above, a man and woman are walking with their children. The man looks down over the railing. "See anything interesting?" he asks.

"The usual," I answer. "A couple of red-winged blackbirds, some killdeer . . ." My voice trails off, and I shrug.

He nods knowingly and raises his hand. I wave back and slow my pace, giving them time to walk away, while I study my own footprints coming toward me in the sand.

5   *Of Legendary Worth*

Rita Johnson and I stood on the Platte's south bank, on land her grandfather John Meyers once owned. "I'm very proud of it," she said. "I never thought I would ever live here." Because of her pride in her grandfather's farm, Rita had given most of it away. A retired farmer who had managed things on her own in the decade since her husband's death, Rita was a large, square-shouldered woman with a no-nonsense demeanor — somewhat gruff but still friendly and open. Open enough to take me, a virtual stranger, around the Meyers Homestead Preserve for a brief tour.

"Grandpa came from a place on the Danube," she said. Kiefer-holz, Germany. She had visited once, to see her ancestors' land. "It looked flat, like this, so I think that's why he chose this spot."

Looking upstream and down, at the reed-choked islands and the wall of dogwoods and willows along the bank, I could only guess that when she said, "this," she meant the Platte as it used to be and not as it looked that day. Rita, who was born in 1924, went on to tell me how the river looked and acted during her childhood, when her family made weekly visits for Grandma Meyers's Sunday dinners. Her memories predated the Kingsley Dam's completion in 1941, when Lake McConaughy began to fill with water for the Tri-County Irrigation Project. That meant she could also recall the river before the Glendo Dam on the North Platte and probably before the Seminoe and Alcova dams as well. She would have been thirteen the first time the state of Nebraska sued Wyoming over North Platte water. Even when she was a child, she said, the river ran dry — or nearly dry — every summer: "They'd put straw down so you could cross the riverbed to go to town." But the spring brought overwhelming floods. "I've seen water from out here," she pointed to our feet, "up to where the interstate is."

Water like that kept the floodplain and river open and free of trees and brush — like the river in Rita's memory. When Rita's father, Carl, was growing up, she told me, this stretch of the river had no trees or shrubs at all. In the winter, Carl and his three brothers could skate as far as Fort Kearny and back on an uninterrupted expanse of ice. It sounded picturesque, but I shuddered inwardly, picturing Willa Cather's fictional heroine Lucy Gayheart, who drowned in the Platte when its dubious ice gave way beneath her and her skate wedged in a flood-borne snag. Cather's Platte River is impetuous and untrustworthy: "This was before the days of irrigation from the Platte; it was then a formidable river in flood time. During the spring freshets it sometimes cut out a new channel in the soft farm land along its banks and changed its bed altogether." The Meyers boys — and Lucy — skated down the Platte just ahead of the wave of big-irrigation projects that fundamentally altered the river from its headwaters to its mouth.

Rita pointed to a row of wooden pilings just upstream from

where we stood. "There used to be a wood bridge there," she said. Looking at the line of pilings and mentally extending them northward, I envisioned the mile-long bridge that appears in some history books and guessed that it had led to Kearney's once-grand Central Avenue.

We walked the quarter mile back to Rita's pickup truck along the tree-bowered dirt track that not so long ago led to the heart of a city that, like many Midwestern communities in the nineteenth century, saw itself as a contender for future capital of the United States.

When John Meyers arrived here shortly after the Civil War, Fort Kearny was still standing four miles downstream, but it would soon follow the covered wagons of the Oregon Trail into history's twilight. Travelers and freight were rumbling across Nebraska on a new form of transportation — the railroad tracks that John and many of his fellow immigrant-homesteaders had helped to build. The new railroad town of Kearney — misspelled namesake of the Fort and its founder, Col. Stephen Watts Kearny — was taking root north of the river as John built his sod house, planted trees, and worked his new farm, including lush riparian pasture land.

In the early 1880s, when he was nearly forty, John married Louise, a young hatmaker living in Kearney, and took her home to a house made from prairie sod "bricks," where their first two sons were born. They moved from the roadside soddy in 1887, into a wood-frame house that was thirty feet by thirty feet and still stands today — as the center room in Rita's big white colonial-style house.

Earlier that day, sitting at the farmhouse kitchen table, Rita had told me stories that had been handed down to her about the farm. Carl told her he had found wheel ruts from pioneer wagons in the unplowed hay meadow. There were rumors about unmarked Oregon Trail graves that a "grave witcher" from Iowa claimed to have located in the cornfield. And I heard about three black walnut trees — now long gone — beneath which Rita once found a scattering of square nails, all that remained of a "dirty-women's ranch" that had served Fort Kearny's disreputable neighbor, Dobytown. In addition to telling his daughter about the farm's history, Carl conveyed his wish for the future: "He said he would like it never to be sold," Rita said resolutely.

With four sons, John Meyers must have thought the family farm's future was assured. But only Carl married. He had two daughters, and the following generation was even smaller, consisting only of Rita's niece, who has never lived in Nebraska and will not likely leave her life and career back east to become a farmer.

That makes Rita the end of the line, and it fell to her to ensure that her grandfather's legacy didn't become a subdivision or a gravel mine. Eventually, she and her niece found an attorney to guide them through the process of creating an educational foundation, to which they donated 320 acres along the Platte. They kept back eighty acres around the house and farmstead. Rita wants the foundation land to be a place for science classes and other school groups to visit. She expected people to be shocked at her giving up such a valuable piece of land; she still seems slightly amazed about it herself: "I thought the men in the white coats would be after me the next day," she said. "But you know, some things are better than money."

The pickup truck turned north on a straight dirt track between shoulder-high rows of corn. Rita explained that she leases some of the foundation land to farmers who raise corn and alfalfa, and she lets other farmers mow the hay meadow each year. So long as part of the land is farmed, the foundation is self-supporting. We bump-bumped along the track toward a dense stand of cottonwoods and up to a gate. "I don't want to drive on the alfalfa, so we'll stop here," she explained. Evidently, she didn't want to walk on the alfalfa either, so although I longed to jump out and explore, I sat in the truck and we looked through the windshield. Nodding toward the trees, I asked if it was very far to the channel. "That's just seep water in there," she said. I had never heard the term but could guess: the rills in the sand, formed by abandoned channels, filled up whenever the groundwater was high. If ever it got high enough and the trees were gone, the channels might connect with each other, and the water might actually flow.

Before us was the twenty-acre alfalfa field, a swatch of rich green between cottonwood bottomlands and corn. As at the river, barn swallows swooped about, scooping up insects. Sandhill cranes like alfalfa fields, too, Rita told me. This field is visible from her house in the spring, when the corn is down. "I can just sit by my barn and watch the cranes dance," she said.

Beyond the alfalfa was the hay meadow, a mere shred of the vast tallgrass prairie traversed by the Oregon Trail pioneers. Rita said she could remember when the land around here raised cattle, not corn, and the grass stretched for miles, east, west, and south. "Anymore, if you see grassland, you know who owns it, because nobody owns it but me."

As we drove out of the corn and back toward Rita's house, my attention wandered to a half-remembered passage, not from *Lucy Gayheart* but from another Willa Cather novel. At home I pulled *O Pioneers!* from the shelf and opened it to the last page, where Alexandra, the middle-aged and childless owner of her family's farm, tells her fiancé Carl that it matters little whether her nephews inherit her land: "The land belongs to the future, Carl; that's the way it seems to me. How many of the names on the county clerk's plat will be there in fifty years? I might as well try to will the sunset over there to my brother's children. We come and go, but the land is always here."

Here in the Medicine Bow Mountains of Wyoming, nearly a mile above the altitude of Kearney County's cornfields, I look down at a white lather of water galloping beneath a sheer bank of evergreens and through a rocky gorge. The name on the map says "North Platte," but this river is as unrecognizable to me as Cinderella must have been to her step-sisters when she danced past them at the ball. Somewhere between here and Nebraska, the clock struck midnight.

Downstream, the canyon gives way to a scrubland valley. It's less steep, with a gravel footpath that's probably easy walking. I turn upstream instead, to the indistinct path toward the canyon, the conifers, and a smooth pillar of stone that resembles a sea stack. The path dips to a sheltered spot at the river's edge, where the water laps through emergent grass and soaks a patch of golden sand. I halt and hold my breath at the sight of what covers the sand: swallowtail butterflies, a score of them at least, their big yellow-and-black wings upright as they tiptoe around. Occasionally, one rises a foot or two in a brief flutter, but mostly they seem engrossed in a feast. A few feet away, drinking at a separate sandy patch, are thirty or more dotted-blue butterflies. Their tiny wings, the size of fingertips, totter as they walk about.

I circle around the butterflies' feeding grounds and find the path again where it rises between shrubs and rocks and then boulders. Easing myself over one boulder and dropping to the next one two feet down, I briefly imagine I'm hiking on the treacherous and beautiful coast of Newfoundland, my birthplace, which I regularly visit. The similarity is not just in the conifers and "sea stack" but in the muted terror I feel whenever I realize that a careless step in pursuit of wonder could instead spell a quick end to my final hike. A gap-toothed fringe of trees is all that stands between me and the rushing, rock-bottomed torrent below. This is the North Platte, I remind myself incredulously, as water pours around and over boulders whose still-rough edges suggest they fell just recently from the canyon wall. But what is "recent" in a place like this? Within my lifetime? That's a brief nothingness. I suppose that in the span required for melting snow to carve a canyon, one human life is a few millimeters, at best.

To the canyon I am nothing. But I feel differently, and so might my family. So it's unfortunate that the path forward is suddenly invisible, and the way back seems to have vanished as well. I stand still for a moment, pretending that I am just enjoying the view. Then, choosing the only direction that's certain, I sit, slide, and aim for a solid-looking tree on the precipice, slowing my descent with any clumps of grass that come to hand. After a few long seconds, my feet brake against the base of the tree's trunk, and I lie against the slope, catching my breath. Then I scramble downstream, angling upward, until the path reappears.

It's time to head for the car anyway. My time is short, and what I have really come to see is miles south yet, in Colorado. I am here to see the snow that melts to form the Platte River. It sounds silly, but after several years of telling visitors at Rowe Sanctuary that the Platte River flows from the Rocky Mountains' snowmelt, I wanted to see the proof.

Besides, in the few minutes that I have been walking, the morning's clear blue sky has gathered a mass of clouds, first white, then pale gray, and now heaped-up pewter-colored thunderheads.

Where the path dips to the river's edge, the butterflies have taken flight. Little eddies of swallowtails twirl about me so closely I expect them to brush against my arms or face. Sometimes the reward for a walk appears after you stop looking. I had thought to stand on a rock in Muir-like ecstasy, above a shouting torrent. Instead, these silent creatures briefly still the river's voice as they trace my outline in the air. The fluttering cloud lasts barely a minute but casts a charm that may last the rest of my life.

The butterflies fly off in all directions. A moment later I feel something that actually touches my skin — a fat raindrop and then another. I reach the car and jump inside with seconds to spare. Rain hammers the roof and hood and sluices down the windows. I can't see the river but can picture raindrops splashing on the banks, around the rocks, and into the channel to mingle with the melted snow that flows from the mountains, supposedly toward the central Platte.

Even before the North Platte was transformed by irrigation, natural forces like seepage and evaporation made it unlikely that a raindrop falling in this canyon would make the long trip to Kearney County to float past John Meyers's homestead.

Today, it seems nearly impossible. A raindrop that splashes into the North Platte River in the Medicine Bow Mountains would have to make its way past six major reservoirs and the dams that contain them, not to mention an assortment of smaller dams and reservoirs.

At each reservoir, a drop of water faces one of four likely

fates: it might flow into an irrigation canal; it might evaporate; it could seep into the ground; or it might be released downstream through the dam, probably powering a hydroelectric plant along the way.

A drop of water that flows into an irrigation canal also faces one of four likely fates: it might evaporate or seep into the ground, either in the canal or in the field; it might run off the field as excess; or it might enter the roots of a plant, like corn or alfalfa.

Water that evaporates, from the river, from reservoirs, from irrigation canals, center pivots, crop fields, and plant leaves, will eventually fall as rain — someplace else.

Water that either seeps into the ground or runs off might eventually reach the river again as "return flow" and resume its journey downstream.

Water that enters a growing plant might later evaporate — a process call transpiration; it might be extracted after harvest when the crop is dried; or it might enter the body of whatever or whoever eats the crop.

Any raindrops that are released from the first reservoir and reach the second one, again, face four possible fates.

If a raindrop did make the journey to Kearney County, it might take years to do so, even if it flowed simply from one reservoir to the next. Reservoirs are like storage vaults or cash boxes where water can be stashed from fall to spring and then withdrawn when growing crops need it. Each reservoir keeps some water as a reserve, stashed from one year to the next.

The quantities are huge, unthinkable. The capacity of just the six largest reservoirs on the North Platte River — Seminoe, Pathfinder, Alcova, Glendo, Guernsey, and McConaughy — is over 4.8 million acre feet, enough to cover the entire state of Nebraska with more than an inch of water.

The rain lets up, and by the time I reach the state line, the sun peeks out between gray cumulus clouds, casting a moody, soggy light over a jewel-green glen. To the right, motion in the grass catches my eye, and I turn just in time to see a golden eagle rise from the grass, beating the air with its seven-foot wings. Beneath the eagle a gentle-looking stream twists through the grasses and under a bridge that's little more than a culvert. I read a small green sign with surprise and think, "This is the North Platte?"

A few minutes later I check the map on the car seat beside me and turn from the quiet highway onto an even emptier road, which takes me to a broad, flat parkland ringed by snow-covered mountains. Beside the road a small farmstead looks drenched in the valley's peacefulness. The road traverses a wet meadow, where water glistens among the green and gray grasses flecked with the pale purple of wild irises. A mallard skims past and drops down into the water and grass. A red-winged blackbird clings to a stalk and creaks out his song. The road crosses a marshy, slow-moving stream, where a cinnamon teal paddles about. There's no sign, but as I look around, this time I am able to believe, "Here is the North Platte."

The Platte River's other tributary, the South Platte, looks broad and vigorous at Greeley, Colorado, where several channels rush among sandbars. Upstream from Greeley, and again downstream, the river gets boosted by inflows from the Bureau of Reclamation's Colorado–Big Thompson Project (C-BT). Built in the 1950s to supplement the South Platte's erratic flows through an agricultural region that depends heavily on irrigation, the

C-BT transfers water from the Colorado River basin, west of the Continental Divide, through tunnels beneath the mountains, downhill through a stair-step series of reservoirs and hydroelectric plants, and through canals and South Platte tributaries to communities and irrigators on this side of the Rockies.

It is almost too fantastic to comprehend, but the result near Greeley is a river that looks fairly unremarkable. In fact, it resembles familiar stretches of the central Platte. Driving east onto Highway 34, I get a second look at the intertwined channels, sandbars, and banks lined with shrubs. Then the river bends north, and I lose sight of it for several miles. Just as I start to worry that I made a mistake, turned the wrong way, and lost the river, it reappears in the valley below the highway — not the water but a green ribbon of trees indicating the presence of water. That's how I am accustomed to locating the Platte. I smile and say, "Well, hello," as if greeting a friend of long acquaintance. For in one sense, I have known the South Platte since birth.

Yesterday afternoon, hours after leaving the North Platte, I pulled off the road north of Fairplay, Colorado, within a mile of the Great Divide. Water streamed in a white froth down the side of a snow-splotched mountain, into the Montgomery Reservoir far, far below, at the beginning of the Middle Fork of the South Platte River. The stream looped and wound south through the valley. An hour later, within that deep valley, I listened to water trickling down the hillside toward the young river that rushed noisily over its rocky bed. A small dam, the second dam in the river's first four miles, formed a little pond, and a trout leapt from the still water. A beaver paddled across, its square nose jutting above, carving a long V-shaped wake. How fitting, I thought, that the cluster of homes upstream was named Placer Valley, calling to mind the Spanish word for "pleasure." It was not perfect, I reflected, as I hopped across a pile of concrete rubble. The long ridges of gravel heaped in the river just downstream marred the river's appearance. Still, a walk in a valley with wild irises and mountain bluebirds was pleasure enough.

Reading a book later in my Fairplay motel room, I discovered my mistake: "placer" is in fact a term for mineral deposits — namely gold — that accumulate in the alluvium of some fast-moving streams. It also refers to the type of mining that involves scooping out the alluvium to retrieve that mineral and discarding the leftover rubble. In Fairplay's wild and wooly gold-rush days, prospectors mined with pans. But in later years machines churned up the riverbed and left long gravel ridges, or tailings, behind.

This morning, after leaving Fairplay, I drove to Eleven Mile Canyon, in the Pike National Forest southwest of Denver. I was curious to see the downstream effect of the Eleven Mile Dam, which captures water for the city of Denver and its environs. I paid the six-dollar entry fee to the U.S. Forest Service and continued down a narrow dirt road that was little more than a ledge on the canyon wall above the South Platte. Spruce trees and boulders shaded the banks; behind many of those boulders, or in the tumbling rapids, stood fly-fishing anglers.

I looked about and wondered, "If a river is this lovely below a dam, what's the harm?"

About eight miles in I found the Eleven Mile Dam. It was an elegant, curved structure, 135 feet high, that, even viewed through a chain-link fence, was pleasing to the eye. A sign informed me that, at nearly one hundred thousand acre-feet, the Eleven Mile Reservoir was the second largest in Denver Water's collection and storage system. One hundred thousand acre-feet is by no means small. But it is less than half the size of Dillon Reservoir, which captures west-slope water for Denver, and it is also less than half the amount of water the Colorado–Big Thompson Project annually transfers from the west slope to Colorado's northeastern counties.

Indeed, the Eleven Mile Reservoir might have looked quite small if Denver Water had succeeded with its plans in the 1980s to build Two Forks Dam, which would have impounded up to 1.1 million acre-feet of the South Platte's waters and more than doubled the utility's storage capacity. Two Forks would have had other effects, as well. In 1990 the EPA vetoed the dam, which would have destroyed a world-class trout stream in Colorado and threatened critical habitat downstream on the central Platte River.

Destroyed instead were the Denver Water Board's long-term sourcing plans, leaving the water utility to reevaluate how to provide water for one of the country's fastest growing cities and its suburbs.

Thirty miles northeast of Eleven Mile Canyon, on my way to Denver, I drove beside the South Platte near the community of Deckers. The river was a glittering, leaping stream that wound north-northeast through open woods. A deer and fawn ambled across the road in front of me. Turkeys strutted in a meadow. At roadside parks along my route, families were fishing and picnicking. The sunny green valley was just a portion of the area that would have been under the waters of a Two Forks Reservoir.

A short while later, in Denver, I stretched my legs with a walk at Overland Pond Park, near the southern end of the South Platte River Greenway. The greenway is a ten-mile-long chain of riverside parks and public spaces connected by a bicycle path — and by a community vision for the South Platte. The Greenway Foundation, created in 1974, has raised private and public funds to clean up the river, build and improve parks, promote outdoor education for youngsters, and build the bike path — all in the interest of transforming the South Platte River from an urban disgrace into an asset. The many cyclists who passed me on the path seemed an indication of the project's success.

They were also evidence that even in the West, where a river is a coveted source of municipal and irrigation water, it has other values, intangible though they may be. If a ten-mile path ran through the dead-dry heart of a city, how many cyclists and joggers would flock to it? Far fewer, I think. As Herman Melville's Ishmael observed, we are drawn to water: "Let the most absent-minded of men be plunged in his deepest reveries — stand that man on his legs, set his feet a-going, and he will infallibly lead you to water, if water there be in all that region."

There is water east of Greeley — certainly more than I found as I drove up U.S. 85 through the irrigated agricultural lands north of Denver. Every few miles, as I drove through Weld County, I left the highway to search out the river; by the time I reached Platteville, I expected it to disappear altogether. Now, driving northeast on I-76 and looking down at the South Platte, I have the feeling there's more river on the fields than in the channel. Between the road and the ribbon of trees is a checkerboard of green circles. For mile after mile, the fields here are watered by center-pivot irrigation. The humpbacked sprinkler systems look like the skeletons of mythological beasts — sea serpents, maybe, or water-breathing dragons.

In central Logan County, weary of the interstate's monotony,

I begin to weave a route that crosses back and forth across the river at each town, a few miles on the state highway north of the river and parallel to the Union Pacific tracks, then a few miles on I-76 south of the river, and then back again. The view at most bridge crossings in the middle of irrigation season shows three snaking channels, often far enough apart to require three separate bridges. In one channel, or perhaps in two, a steady stream flows around former sandbars — now islands anchored by small aspens and purple loosestrife. In most places, the southernmost channel is scarcely a channel at all — just a forested bottomland with little or no visible water.

The sun is setting as I cross the Nebraska state line. Green exit signs flash past every few miles, glowing in my headlights. I see a sign for Ogallala and the road to the Kingsley and Keystone Dams; next is Paxton, where the Sutherland Canal carries North Platte water *under* the South Platte, under I-80, and then east to the Sutherland Reservoir. The next exit is for the city of Sutherland and the reservoir itself, which stores Platte River water to cool the coal-fired Gerald Gentleman Station electric plant. Twenty miles past Sutherland is the city of North Platte, just upstream from the confluence of the North and South Platte Rivers and the dam that shunts water into the Tri-County Canal. After powering three hydro plants along the Tri-County Canal, the Platte's water will course through a labyrinth of irrigation canals and laterals . . . and the green signs keep coming.

I delude myself if I say that I know this river like an old friend. On this dark road I feel like an acquaintance, at best. Engineers know this river. Accountants and lawyers might know who owns the water. As for myself, I just know what I see. I'm ready to get home. Maybe tomorrow I'll find a quiet place to take a walk and see what the birds along the Platte are doing.

At six thirty in the morning in late July, the birds are all awake and busy at the Meyers Homestead Preserve. House wrens chatter frenetically in the dense tree line that marks the edge of the bottomland. Somewhere a song sparrow sings, "*twee-ee, twee-ee, tiddle-iddle*." Two bluebirds — one with the speckled breast of a young fledgling — fly down from a low branch. Their wings briefly flutter side by side in the alfalfa before they fly together back up to the branch. It looks like hunting lessons. The sky is clear except for the silver disk of the full moon and the rickety-flitting silhouettes of two chimney swifts.

Across the field are the deer and turkeys that Rita said I would see. She didn't say there would be so many: besides the two puffed-up gobblers fanning their tails, I count fifteen turkeys foraging in the alfalfa, though I can't be sure because the pullets — like the youngsters of so many species — won't hold still long enough for counting. Near the turkeys a herd of twenty deer graze; a fawn bursts from the trees and gallops past the adults, into the field of tall corn. It's apparently no cause for alarm. The adults don't even raise their heads. Kids.

If it weren't for the steady wind blowing at twenty miles an hour from the southeast, this would look like an idyllic scene from a fairy tale. But wind is one of the great realities of the Great Plains.

For a few minutes, I walk the tree line — a mix of enormous cottonwoods, mulberries, and a thick fringe of phragmites and ditch weed, marijuana's wild-growing cousin. The wind rattles the cottonwood leaves, making a rushing sound like falling rain. At a spot where the ditch weed thins slightly, I plunge in, then down a short slope to the dry bottomland, and through thigh-high weeds and grasses and mature cottonwood trees. Some of the more ancient trees have collapsed; I crawl over a trunk and through a few fallen limbs, thinking, "There's a river here somewhere." Next I climb up a low sandy ridge of cedars and saplings and then down again through a dense stand of phragmites that towers over my head. I emerge to find a tiny, slow-moving channel — so slow moving that algae cling to the edges. It's too wide to leap across, and my rubber boots are at home in the garage. But the water is clear and the gravel bottom, firm looking; so repeating the mantra of the ill prepared — "It's only water" — I take two quick steps across. Next is a thicket of sandbar willows and then a ridge covered with coarse gravel, in sharp contrast to the silky sand everywhere else. I stoop to pick up a stone the size and shape of a goose egg. A stone. They're not so common in sand-and-loess-covered central Nebraska. Turning it over in my hand, I try to picture the distance it has traveled and imagine the force of the flood that could polish three-inch rocks and sweep them to a ridge that is now high and dry. I slip the rock into my pocket and skid down a swale and then over one more ridge, where I find the river at last. The banks are covered with cedars, willows, and a strip of phragmites. The water is surprisingly broad and weaves among sandbars. I'm looking down, wondering if the stream is very deep, when I hear, "*crash, crash, crash*," in the brush. A doe bursts out and leaps into the water, which comes up only to her ankles. Once in the water, she slows and prances with high, dainty steps to the nearest sandbar and then crosses to the far bank.

After a few minutes by the water, I turn around and retrace my up-and-down course through abandoned river channels and dry sloughs. Emerging from trees at the edge of the hay meadow, I expect to find the same tallgrass prairie plants I have found in other Platte valley meadows. But this field is sparser and much drier than other native meadows I have seen — and no wonder. The river is now a quarter mile away and several feet lower than its former floodplain. Between the whorled milkweed, prairie coneflowers, and Indian grass is bare sand. It tells me two things: that the river once flowed here and that it has been dry for many years. Here and there, I find small clumps of moisture-loving plants: prairie cordgrass and shoots of horsetail. It's as if the land holds a memory of having been a wet meadow, but the memory is fading.

Tonight, sitting at my desk, I hold the egg-shaped stone in my hand, rubbing the nearly smooth surface with my thumb and thinking about Rita and her grandfather's homestead. In a country where we talk of starter homes, trading up, and retirement villages, fewer and fewer of us share Rita's experience. She literally walks in her father's and grandfather's footsteps, sees the sun set at the same angle as they saw it. She sees the same river they saw, altered though it may be. She keeps them in that place. If I owned a piece of land where my ancestors had walked daily, coaxed new crops from the ground, and built a house and barn with their own hands, wouldn't I do everything in my power to preserve their legacy? If the ground needed more water, wouldn't I look for a way to get it?

The last time I saw Rita, she seemed to have a lot on her mind, but not so much that she failed to point out the robust growth of her tenant's corn as we drove past. "That will have tassels soon," she said with satisfaction, musing that it had grown better than some neighbors had predicted when the tenant used a no-till method to plant. Rita seems to be accustomed to challenging people's expectations. She implied that when her husband, Orian, died in 1995, there were plenty of people who thought a woman left to farm on her own might not make it.

"I'm going to a meeting tonight," she said, "with those weed people, and I bet I'll be the only woman there." She was referring to a group of organizations that have teamed up to help river-front landowners combat the invasion of phragmites. I waited, wondering if she would elaborate or say what she planned to do. But she was thinking about much more than weed control. She spoke of her niece, who is John Meyers's last remaining heir, after Rita. They had been talking about the future of the house and farmstead. "She said, for all she cares, I can sell the place," Rita said, sounding sad and frustrated. "She just doesn't know its *value*. Not money . . . but the love that went into it."

I felt like I was standing in line at a wake, not knowing what to say to the surviving family member. Nothing I could say would offer comfort. How does one walk away from the path worn by a grandparent's footprints? My father's father did it when he left the family farm in Switzerland. My mother did it when she left Newfoundland. All the Pawnees did when they left Nebraska. Somehow. We drove in silence for a few minutes. "So," she concluded, "I don't know what I'm going to do."

Willa Cather's Alexandra asked rhetorically, "How many of the names on the county clerk's plat will be there in fifty years?" People have indeed come and gone. But many homesteaders' names are still in the plat book, and their descendants are striving to keep them there.

Rita will make up her own mind about spraying phragmites on her stretch of the river; either way, it is likely to happen someday. If she is cautious, it's because she is doing her best to honor her grandfather's memory and her father's wishes. Someday, the foundation's trustees may decide to mow down the willows and locusts, cut the cottonwoods, run a fire through the meadow, and uncover the river that John Meyers saw when he chose his new home. Whatever they choose to do, the land along the Platte will still be there, and John Meyers's name will be on it, though his heirs will be gone.

6   *River Walkers*

AUGUST AND SEPTEMBER

The north wind blows across I-80 and carries the constant whine of traffic toward the bottomland forest of the Bassway Strip. The cars and semitrucks are a half mile away but sound close enough to mow me down . . . unless the heat kills me first.

Walking along the dusty entrance road, I take a swig from my water bottle and splash some of its contents on my face and neck, knowing even as I do it that the wind will instantly suck the moisture away and leave the hot air sticking to my skin like gauze on a wound. It's half-crazy to walk through a weedy forest in the middle of a ninety-five-degree day. Sometimes I just want to see how much I can stand.

I climb a sand embankment and pick my way along a path choked with sweet clover, ditch weed, and twisting wild grape vines. Hoary vervain, scattered here and there, sends up spindly clumps of ragged, pale-purple flower spikes. Past the ridge, I plunge, reluctantly, down through a bank of trees, mostly cottonwoods and red cedar. Virginia creeper and wild grape sprawl and climb all around.

The shade gives scant relief from the heat, but because the trees block the breeze, mosquitoes begin to buzz around my head and pitch in my hair. I fan my hands about my ears and keep walking.

Somewhere a cardinal is singing, "*purrr-dee, purrr-dee,*" and house wrens are chattering. They only irritate me: woodland birds in the Great American Desert. And besides, should it really be so hard to take a walk beside a prairie stream? The massive trunk of a downed cottonwood blocks my path. I swing one leg over, straddling it, and then swing the other leg over and sit a few seconds on the rough bark, arms crossed, to look around. What this place needs is a good fire.

Some people look at trees in the floodplain and say they are good for diversity — for flycatchers, thrushes, and woodpeckers. I hear this from at least one local biologist, whose learning I respect. Other people, whose sincerity I likewise respect, argue that nature should be allowed to take its course. I disagree. We humans have knocked nature off its course, like a train knocked off its tracks, and it's our job to set things right.

In some ways, this resembles the ordinary eastern forests of my childhood, with green growth and decaying trees — all the good rot from which new life will spring. But amid the leaf litter and fallen branches, where the ground is exposed, I spy Platte River sand. How long has it been since the river flowed here? I take another swig of warm water and trudge on. Near the channel, the weeds thicken into a five-foot-tall swath of phragmites. Just looking at it makes my skin itch. I think briefly that I cannot get through it and then realize that I would simply *rather* not, so I steel myself, take a deep breath, and shoulder through. I can stand anything for five minutes.

But five minutes would in fact be too much. Within just

seconds, I pull up sharply when the ground beneath my feet ends in a three-foot drop straight down to the churning green waters of the north channel. Downstream, the channel bends to the south, and I see where the rushing current has cut into and under the bank, a bank that seems to defy gravity, held up only by the dense roots of phragmites — like the phragmites on which I am standing. I take two steps back.

The channel is fast and deep, with none of the Platte's characteristic sandbars — at least not anymore. This is hungry water — hungry for sediment. Along the river's course, impoundments and constrictions, such as bridge crossings, repeatedly alter the rate at which water flows. When the flow accelerates, it sweeps up sediment, which falls to the riverbed as the water slows down. Influxes of sediment-free water — from municipal treatment plants, for example — increase the river's appetite, which it satisfies by eating up its own bed and banks. In its natural state, the river spilled out of its banks even as it washed them away, flooding backwaters and meadows. Now, deep roots — mostly phragmites' roots — stabilize the banks and islands. As the river flows faster, pinched into a root-stabilized flume, it cuts deeper still. And the deeper it cuts, the more divorced it becomes from the backwaters, wetlands, and wet meadows that were once an integral part of the Platte. Almost nothing here resembles the flat, braiding river channels where cranes roost and shorebirds scurry. Even the sky looks smaller.

Feeling hopeless, I start the weary march back to the road. So many miles of the Platte River are degraded or overgrown. It all seems beyond redemption.

But I know that's not true, because within a few miles of this strip of forest, the middle channel flows broad and flat, with a network of sandbars. The open-channel areas that cranes and other birds seek can still be found along the Big Bend, thanks in part to habitat restoration and maintenance. "Maintenance" is the relatively low-tech practice of disking the riverbed, as if it were a weedy farm field, to churn up the encroaching plant growth.

"Restoration," on the other hand, is more difficult and expensive. The process of making the river's complex systems look and function as they once did requires a blend of technical expertise, creativity, and no small measure of hope.

Land-based conservation organizations, including Rowe Sanctuary, the Crane Trust, and the Nature Conservancy, own or manage thousands of acres along the Big Bend and continue the gradual, years-long process of restoring and then maintaining Platte River habitat, often pooling resources and working cooperatively.

Apart from these groups, the Nebraska Game and Parks Commission owns several tracts of land along the central Platte. Some are recreation areas, popular for camping and cookouts. Others, like the Bassway Strip, offer close-to-town opportunities to hunt white-tailed deer and other game on public land. A few of the state-owned areas — with funding help from private conservation organizations and the state-lottery-funded Nebraska Environmental Trust — have undergone restoration projects that provide just a glimpse of the historic braided river.

By far, the majority of property along the Platte is privately owned, however. Individual farmers, hunters, and landowners, and the decisions they make, are therefore crucial to the Platte River's long-term recovery.

Kenny Dinan and Kirk Schroeder have spent their careers helping private landowners who make the decision to improve habitat on their portions of the Platte. Kenny and Kirk are based in Grand Island and work for the U.S. Fish and Wildlife Service's Partners for Fish and Wildlife program. At the end of a daylong wetland seminar in Hastings, they joined me at the conference center lounge to tell me about their work. Kenny is the Partners' program coordinator for Nebraska, and Kirk is assistant coordinator. While their responsibilities cover the whole state, much of their work, especially Kirk's, has focused on the Platte River.

The Partners program provides assistance, both financial and technical, to private landowners who want to improve habitat on their property. Along the Platte, Kenny and Kirk have worked with over 150 landowners — including farmers and "recreational owners," who use their property mostly for hunting and other outdoor pursuits. They also work cooperatively with the Nature Conservancy, the Crane Trust, Rowe Sanctuary, and most recently, the Platte River Recovery Implementation Program.

"So many species rely on this system," said Kenny. "It's not just restoration for its own sake." Restoration along the Platte River can have many meanings and many phases. The first Partners' projects were limited to channel clearing — cutting trees, brush, and weeds from the riverbed, islands, and banks. But complete habitat restoration calls for restoring — or sometimes re-creating — a complex, integrated system of open channels, sandbars and low islands, backwater sloughs, and wet meadows.

In the early 1990s Kenny and Kirk began to construct backwater sloughs — areas of slow or standing water that are "hydrologically connected" to the river through groundwater flows but are outside the current. One of the first efforts was a series of sloughs at Rowe Sanctuary. North of the main channel but still within the riverbed, the sloughs were created with excavation equipment to remove riverbed sand — just deep enough to intersect with the water table. The reexposed groundwater generally percolates into the sloughs all summer, providing water for wildlife even when surface flows have dried up. In the winter the relatively warm groundwater keeps the sloughs open when the rest of the river is frozen, so overwintering waterfowl have a place to roost.

Later projects included wet-meadow restorations — re-creating wetlands in abandoned channels and reestablishing native plant communities. And most recently Kenny and Kirk have recontoured river channels to build nesting islands for least terns and piping plovers.

Habitat restoration on the Platte is both a science and an art. They take pride, Kirk told me, in visiting or flying over a completed project, like a restored meadow, after five years and being able to say, "You can't tell that this meadow hasn't always been here."

Their goal, they tell me, is to restore substantial areas of habitat within each bridge segment — the six- to twelve-mile stretches between bridge crossings — along the river. Usually the process starts with a conservation organization that owns a large parcel in a given bridge segment. After a flagship project is finished and the results become apparent, neighboring landowners begin to follow along.

Often, the "restoration curve" with an individual landowner emulates the learning curve Kenny and Kirk have followed. Initially, some landowners — especially those who are not wholly at ease working with conservation organizations or a federal agency — just agree to clear trees and brush and to disc the phragmites. As their confidence grows, they may decide next to build backwater sloughs.

"When you look at how the river was historically, sloughs have become the missing component," said Kirk, "so that's one thing we're focusing on."

In a more complete restoration, wet meadows and reshaped channels come next. Where did they get their ideas and learn what it takes to build a slough, reshape a channel, or position an island? Mostly, they relied on intuition and their understanding of the river and taught themselves. "No one had done that kind of work before," Kenny said. The first sloughs they built were relatively small; as their experience lengthened, so did the sloughs. Now, with over fifty miles of sloughs along the central Platte, they have built some that are a mile or more in length. As for what makes the lightbulb turn on, Kenny said, "Usually it happens when you're standing in the river."

Both attended the geomorphology classes required by the Fish and Wildlife Service, but only after they had been doing restoration work for some time. Kirk said, "We can do the mathematical calculations, but . . ." He tipped his head slightly and shrugged.

I asked them whether it was difficult to gain a landowner's confidence and get the go-ahead to bring in earthmoving equipment. "If we can bring them an old aerial photo to show them what the river used to look like," said Kenny, "it's a pretty easy sell."

A few weeks after our first conversation, wanting a look at Kirk's collection of aerial photos, I dropped by his office in Grand Island's Federal Building. The hundred-year-old structure was once the city's magnificent post office and courthouse. Its cornices and decorative moldings now lie buried under the retrofittings for modern necessities like ductwork and telephone wires, and the building seems to be in a permanent state of renovation. No wonder Kirk and Kenny prefer to be out in the river. Their offices are on opposite sides of an echoing stairwell, but in Kirk's office there's no room for an echo. It's jammed with heavy, industrial-looking furniture, maps, and binders. In the corner is a lawyer's cabinet filled with soil maps. Charts and map boards lean against a wall. Clearly, even intuitive work requires a great deal of reference material.

Kirk pulled a banker's box from under the table. "They were about to throw these away," he said as he hefted the box onto the tabletop. "These" were photographs from the federal government's first aerial-photo survey of the Platte River in the late 1930s.

Kirk sorted through the photos, pointing out locations that he assumed I would recognize, but some places looked unbelievably different: mile after mile of broad, interwoven channels, treeless banks, broad meadows streaked with wetlands. I remarked on the near absence of trees and shrubs; Kirk agreed, observing that the growth of woody plants had really taken off in the last forty years. "But the biggest change," Kirk said, "is not the woody growth but how incised the river has gotten." Landowners recognize the change, too, he said. "They know that when a river is incised, all of a sudden it gets deeper and faster."

The incising affects different landowners — from hunters to homesteaders' descendants — in different ways. Some turn to Kirk for a solution. Owners of a farm near Elm Creek called him about the narrowing channel and encroaching trees that had drastically changed the place's appearance in the hundred years that the family had lived there. The view to the north had shrunk to just a quarter mile, but the family's matriarch could remember looking out across the valley as a child, to the railroad track and passing trains. Mom wanted her children and grandchildren to enjoy that same vista.

Closer to Grand Island was a farmer whose concerns were more pragmatic. His channels were becoming choked with phragmites, and he could see the trouble ahead: "He knows where that water's going to go when it floods," Kirk said.

Waterfowl hunters, too, have observed the benefits of river restoration. "I've had guys come up to me when I was out standing in the water," said Kirk. They had watched ducks and geese flying into restored areas and recognized that they could improve habitat on their own stretch of the river.

Still, all these individual projects are just pieces in a huge mosaic that must somehow be assembled into a picture that makes sense and holds together.

"If we want to have any longevity to maintaining the river system," Kirk told me, "we need something that's simple, cost effective, and, to the extent possible, maintains itself."

In centuries past, the river did maintain itself with sediment-laden, channel-scouring flows and periodic high-water surges. Conservationists have argued in recent decades that properly timed releases of water from reservoirs — what they call "pulses" — could emulate that effect. But before a pulse is even possible, miles and miles of channel-choking plant growth — including phragmites, willows, cottonwoods, and other trees — must be killed and cleared away. Thick stands of vegetation not only create bottlenecks; they guzzle scarce water and trap sediment among their roots.

"Water and sediment are what that river *is*," Kirk told me. "You totally change the physical characteristics of the Platte if you lose either one of them." Invasive plants rob the river of both.

Removal of phragmites and other invading plants would be

the first step in a technique that restoration advocates call "clear/level/pulse." They envision that once channels are cleared of weeds and shrubs and are mechanically flattened out — a reversal of incising — pulse flows could be sent down the river. These high-volume releases from reservoirs, the argument goes, would transport masses of sediment that would help the river once again maintain its channels and sandbars. But that returns to the problem of phragmites, willows, and other plants whose thick roots have transformed sandbars into stable islands. Eventually, said Kirk, "to get back to where we're transporting sediment, we have to mobilize those islands again." The answer to whether clear/level/pulse will work, or even be entirely feasible, may be years in the future. In any case, Kirk suspects mechanical treatment methods, like tree cutting or disking, are here to stay. And he will keep working with landowners who want to change their own stretches of the river.

The Partners for Fish and Wildlife program is just one of many entities involved in habitat management and restoration along the Platte. Working cooperatively and through partnerships, agencies and organizations share their ideas, equipment, grant funds, and even staff positions. Kirk calls it, "the largest riverine restoration and management project anywhere in the country."

Before the 1970s nobody was talking about restoring channels and wetlands along the Platte River or protecting wildlife habitat. For most of Nebraska's history, people in rural areas had their hands full protecting *human* habitat and making a living. "Conservation" on the Platte and its tributaries meant harnessing scarce water and putting it to good use, rather than letting it go to waste in the Gulf of Mexico. That meant engineering new water development projects to capture, store, and distribute whatever came downstream.

The beginnings of wildlife and habitat protection along the central Platte came in response to the plans for one such development project, the Nebraska Mid-State Reclamation Project, which wildlife biologist Charles Frith had recognized in the late 1960s as a mortal threat to the river's wildlife habitat.

Mid-State would have diverted the Platte's surplus flows (meaning any water that was not already subject to a prior claim) from an outlet near Lexington, at the west of the Platte's Big Bend, into several off-stream reservoirs north of the river. The project's original purpose was to store irrigation water. Later plans emphasized additional benefits, including hydroelectric power, flood control, recreation, and "groundwater recharge," meaning that water from the river — surface water — would be allowed to seep into the aquifer to offset the effects of groundwater irrigation. In any case, opponents feared that Mid-State would remove nearly all the remaining water from the central Platte — the portion of the river on which cranes and other waterbirds were most dependent.

When Frith began his research, he approached the National Audubon Society in search of financial assistance. Upon learning of the Mid-State plan, Audubon responded with much more than research funding.

They sent their newly hired regional director, Ron Klataske, a wildlife biologist by training but an activist by nature. Klataske got to know the river; then he got to know local newspaper editors and outdoor writers. He organized Audubon chapters in Nebraska. And he went door-to-door along the Big Bend, getting to know all the farmers who owned land on the river segments where Frith had found the best habitat. That was because Audubon was also prepared to send something else: the bulk of a bequest from a New Jersey psychologist and bird lover named Lillian Annette Rowe. Dr. Rowe had directed that the money be used to acquire land for a bird sanctuary. After months of kitchen-table discussions, Klataske found several landowners who were willing to sell.

In 1973 the National Audubon Society announced that it had purchased options on 445 acres of riverfront land in Buffalo County south of Gibbon. The location of their purchase was based in part on Frith's data and advice. Meanwhile, Audubon chapters in Kearney, Grand Island, Hastings, and Lincoln banded together with other supporters, including a few of Frith's Kearney State College professors, to form a group called Save the Platte. They began a grassroots information campaign, with mailings, public meetings, and occasional hand-drawn newspaper ads, to oppose the reclamation project. The Mid-State Reclamation District, supported by the Bureau of Reclamation, launched its own advertising campaign, which dwarfed the efforts of the Audubon groups. But the river and its protectors had allies: a loosely organized group called Mid-State Irrigators, Inc., led by Gibbon farmer Mark Bolin, also opposed the project, arguing that it was overpriced and unnecessary.

Authorization for the project came to a public vote in November 1975, and the majority of voters in the three-county reclamation district said, "No, thank you." The Mid-State developers had not only lost an irrigation project; they had awakened a sleeping giant — or more precisely, a whole clan of sleeping giants who have been guarding the river ever since.

The river's guardians were ready in the late 1970s when the Basin Electric Power Cooperative proposed the Grayrocks Dam and Reservoir Project on Wyoming's Laramie River, a major tributary of the North Platte. The National Audubon Society, National Wildlife Federation, Nebraska Wildlife Federation, and the State of Nebraska sued to stop the project, arguing that by degrading Big Bend habitat, the project threatened the survival of whooping cranes, an endangered species. Grayrocks went forward, but subject to a legal settlement that set aside $7.5 million for creation of the Platte River Whooping Crane Habitat Maintenance Trust, now known simply as the Crane Trust. The Nature Conservancy assisted in the Crane Trust's first land acquisition and also established its own long-term presence in the Platte River valley.

The guardians continued to challenge water development projects, one after another, and sometimes one atop another: Narrows Unit, Prairie Bend, Two Forks, Deer Creek, Catherland. What the river's defenders needed, and what irrigators, municipalities, and the Bureau of Reclamation needed, was a region-wide policy that would streamline the lengthy process of proposing, evaluating, and approving or rejecting the various uses of the Platte's waters. The matter came to a head in the late 1980s when the federal operating license for the Central Nebraska Public Power and Irrigation District was due to expire. The CNPPID, or Central, owns and operates Kingsley Dam and Lake McConaughy, whose 1.75 million-acre-foot storage capacity casts a long shadow over habitat conditions on the Platte River. Central's initial relicensing application in 1984 was rejected for failure to address its operations' impact on endangered species. After a lengthy revision of Central's application, as well as continued disputes over other water projects, the U.S. Fish and Wildlife Service urged that the three states of the Platte River system — Nebraska, Wyoming, and Colorado — plus the U.S. Department of Interior resolve their disagreements with a basin-wide plan. The Federal Energy Regulatory Commission finally approved Central's new license in 1998, pending the eventual creation and adoption of the Platte River Recovery Implementation Program, which the states and the Interior ultimately signed in 2006.

The program, in effect a master plan for wildlife habitat and water use in the Platte River watershed, depends on the willingness of the three states to continue cooperating. In the meantime, it provides a level of legal certainty for water users, and it offers the prospect of tens of millions of federal dollars for research, habitat protection, and restoration. It also provides a framework for cooperation among organizations, agencies, and governments that value the Platte for different reasons. In that way, it echoes that first victory in 1975, when a group of birdwatchers and biologists teamed up with irrigators and set aside their differences to achieve a common goal.

On a breezy afternoon in late September, I walk east along the river toward Rowe Sanctuary's Triplett Trail and the "tower," a two-story observation blind. I take a circuitous route to stay clear of trailers and heavy earthmoving vehicles that are working nearby. Next month, after irrigation season ends, the river will flow again, but September offers a last chance to operate equipment in the nearly dry channels.

I hear the machinery before I can see it, as I walk through the trees and toward the bank, downstream from the work area. In the channel north of the tower blind, workers are preparing to reshape the riverbed and sandbars and to construct nest islands for least terns and piping plovers. I want to see the transformation for myself.

The first part of the job is removal of hundreds of trees — from saplings to thirty-year-old cottonwoods — that are encroaching on the channel. I raise my binoculars toward the yellow machines moving amid the spindly trees. I've seen these contractors in action before — two brothers who specialize in habitat restoration — and I love to watch them work. The bulldozer and backhoe look strangely graceful as they roll to and fro. The bulldozer shoves slowly at a stand of trees and then backs away as they topple over; the backhoe approaches, shovel extended, scoops them up, and gives a little shake, as if it were holding a dust rag, to clean the loose soil from the roots. Then it pivots to add its jawful of trees to a growing pile. They repeat the process over and over, circling around each other. Their motions remind me of the ease with which long-married couples glide around a ballroom floor. The roar of machinery fades from my consciousness, and all I'm aware of is fluid motion ... and a widening, flat riverbank. Hours of tree removal remain. But in a day or two, after the trees are cleared, the next part of the project will begin. The workers will scoop up sand to form sloughs along the channel edges and will rearrange the sandy riverbed to sculpt sandbars and islands of various heights. To discourage weeds, they'll top some islands with heavy gravel — all from the streambed.

Mesmerized, I watch for a long time, but the trees go on and on. Finally, I walk upstream toward the opposite end of the sanctuary, to the area we call the Dinan Tract. The John J. Dinan Memorial Bird Conservation Area was named for Kenny Dinan's late brother, who managed the Non-Game Bird Program of the Nebraska Game and Parks Commission. Rowe Sanctuary worked with Kenny and Kirk through the Partners for Fish and Wildlife program to restore this section of river channel in 2006, in a process similar to the work I just observed. Later, the floodplain was planted with native prairie seed.

Today the sunflowers at the Dinan Tract stand at least a foot above my head but offer no real shade from the pounding sun. Eighty degrees at the end of September. At least the insects are happy. Near the channel restoration, thick-trunked cottonwood trees mark the level to which the river once flowed. One ancient tree overhanging the bank rustles and then flutters. But no, it's not the tree — a golden eagle launches itself from a low branch. Its brown-and-gold wings beat the air a few quick times as it rises, circles, and then flies upstream.

The bank drops off to flat, soft sand and a series of sloughs around which the heavy seed heads of Indian grass, cordgrass, and big bluestem stir in the breeze. A ridge of sand forms a sort of causeway between the two sloughs, and as I cross it, I hear, "*plop, plop, plop, plop.*" I look down to see dozens and dozens of splashes, as leopard frogs, most of them tiny as gumdrops, flee the sound — or perhaps the vibrations — of my approaching footsteps by hopping into the water. "*Plop, plop, plop, plop.*" There must be hundreds of them. Each tiny splash leaves a circle and then a series of concentric, rippling rings that spread and intersect with other rings.

I step over a line of raccoon tracks and roam among the grasses that grow in sparse bunches in the sand. Arms loose at my sides, I let fuzzy-headed grass stalks trail between my fingers. Grasshoppers beat against the legs of my pants, cling briefly, and fall away.

In the spring this might be part of the channel, but right now it's more sand than water. A few rivulets wander around the sandbars and islands midriver. A shaggy great blue heron stands at the edge of one sandbar in the company of dowitchers and yellowlegs, all placid among a group of frantically running killdeer. I watch through binoculars, not wanting to disturb them by venturing closer. Upstream from the heron and shorebirds is a nest island, taller and flatter than the sandbars. Least terns and piping plovers did indeed nest there, starting the first year after the islands were built. Kirk and Kenny had expected that this would be a good spot. "We thought if they were going to nest anywhere on the river," Kenny told me, "they were going to nest at Rowe."

Before these islands were built, tern and plover nest sites in south-central Nebraska had become limited to open-sand areas at sand and gravel mining operations. Quarry operators, to their credit, were accommodating, but the birds still faced disadvantages. For example, terns had to leave their nests and fly to the river for fish to feed their young, and the landlocked sites made them easy targets for predators.

Through binoculars I can see a fuzz of green weeds sprouting on the island. If the weeds grow taller, next year's nesting conditions might not be so good. But that's all right, because the number of nest islands on the central Platte grows every year — there are now dozens — so that birds can choose different islands in different years. That allows them to adapt to conditions, nest where the water and food supply suit them, and keep predators, like raccoons, guessing.

The heron croaks and takes off, alone in the blue expanse of the sky. In half a year, the Dinan Tract will once again be full of a bugling, jostling mass of ten thousand cranes. Today it is full of little frogs and hope. And that feels like plenty.

7   *Flickering Light on the Flyway*

OCTOBER AND EARLY NOVEMBER

And the good south wind still blew behind,
But no sweet bird did follow

SAMUEL TAYLOR COLERIDGE, *Rime of the Ancient Mariner*

A world without whooping cranes. That's what this planet nearly became in the two decades before my birth. Perhaps, if I had never seen that incandescent white against the sky, the seven-foot sweep of black-tipped wings, if I had been born too late, I would not have felt the loss.

For those of us born too late, the idea of a great white bird that haunted long-vanished wetlands across a broad swath of North America might have stirred faint nostalgia. We might have guessed by their name that when pairs of the phantom birds called in unison, their high-pitched voices rent the morning air over a marsh. But to most people, the whooping crane, like the passenger pigeon and great auk, would have been no more than a photograph in a book.

In the 1940s the number of whooping cranes on earth dwindled to about two dozen. Picture two cartons of eggs on the kitchen counter — four rows of six little eggs, one sharp elbow away from destruction. Two wild populations existed. The nonmigrating flock near the Gulf Coast in southwest Louisiana was already doomed. In 1940 only six birds remained — just one row in the egg carton — with no new chicks hatching. The other flock, which migrated through the central flyway of the Great Plains, was faring little better. Of the fourteen to twenty-one birds identified in the early 1940s, usually half or fewer were paired up and successful at rearing a chick that survived until fall migration.

For any species, rare or not, reproduction is the key to long-term survival. Short-lived animals like mice, minnows, and mayflies reproduce copiously and from an early age. Parental care is scant or nonexistent. The copious young die copiously, but many live long enough to produce another generation. At the other end of the spectrum, larger and longer-lived creatures, like humans and elephants, are generally slow to reach sexual maturity; they have a relatively small number offspring, on which they lavish parental care, ensuring that a high percentage reach adulthood. Either way, as long as new life keeps pace with death, the species has a future.

That wasn't happening with whooping cranes. Even before their precipitous decline, the species may have numbered only in the low thousands. Their reproduction rate is slow; birds reach sexual maturity around age four but are often seven years old before they successfully negotiate the process of nest building, incubating a pair of eggs, and caring for chicks, of which at least one usually dies before summer's end.

The term biologists use for the number of newly born or hatched young that survive to maturity is "recruitment." If recruitment matches the rate at which a population's adults die, equilibrium is maintained. But when the natural recruitment rate is low, a slight shift at either end of the life cycle can tip the scales.

In the 1800s the whooping cranes' scales tipped sharply, and the birds began to vanish across their traditional breeding range as human populations swelled in those same areas. Unregulated hunting and specimen collecting took the same toll on whooping cranes as they took on many other bird species. The 1918 Migratory Bird Treaty Act and equivalent legislation in Canada regulated the hunting of migratory game birds and protected nongame birds. But by the time the laws were passed, the dwindling whooping crane population had for many years been losing the battle against a more pervasive and complex threat.

"Habitat loss" is a rather clinical-sounding name for what happens when wild creatures have no place to live their lives. To highly territorial species, like whooping cranes, the loss is especially damaging. Before the westward push of pioneers, whooping cranes' breeding grounds stretched between present-day Edmonton, Alberta, and metro Chicago. Today those parklands and prairie wetlands are covered by corn, wheat, highways, and cities.

Imagine it's the summer of 1847 in a northern county of the brand-new state of Iowa, not far in time or space from the invention of a steel-clad plow blade that finally conquered the tough prairie sod. Now imagine a pair of tall white birds in a sprawling marsh — the same marsh where they have spent every summer for years. They're mounding sodden cattail stalks and rushes into an island-like nest. The marsh's waters are shallow, and the plant growth is sparse, so the cautious cranes can keep an eye out for raccoons and other nest raiders. The water and soil are rich with plant roots, larvae, snails. The air sings with frogs' voices and insect wings. Paradise.

Three weeks later, as the cranes take turns brooding their

two eggs, they hear another sound: human voices. Men are speaking—calling to each other and laughing—as they dig near the marsh. The digging and the voices continue all day, and resume the next day, and the next. But the frightened birds no longer hear. They've abandoned their nest and their territory for an isolated spot that becomes harder and harder to imagine as we picture the human population growing in Iowa, Wisconsin, Minnesota...

Within a few decades the whooping cranes' call vanished from marshes across the plains. Their breeding range contracted northward and westward, to a patch of Canadian taiga just a few hundred miles shy of the Arctic Circle. The last known wintering grounds, at the other end of the cranes' annual life cycle, were along the Texas coast. In between lay a 2,500-mile migration route—25 to 175 percent longer than what whooping cranes had flown a century earlier.

The first intentional step to save the nearly extinct species came in 1937 with creation of the Aransas National Wildlife Refuge near Corpus Christi, Texas. Nominally a waterfowl refuge, it also protected much of the area where whooping cranes spend nearly half the year. In a seminal monograph published by the National Audubon Society in 1952, whooping crane researcher Robert Porter Allen reflected that creation of the Aransas refuge may have been the greatest factor in saving the whooper from extinction. Their breeding range had been unwittingly protected as well in 1922, when Canada's government designated the Wood Buffalo National Park, spanning the border of Alberta and the Northwest Territories, as a preserve for the woodland subspecies of the American bison.

Allen proposed the protection of habitat areas—in particular the Platte River—along the migration route. In addition, he recommended a public-information campaign throughout the central flyway to reduce the likelihood of shootings, whether intentional or accidental.

Throughout the 1940s and most of the 1950s, the numbers of whooping cranes hovered in the vicinity of a fragile two dozen. Then gradually, in fits and starts, the tiny number began to grow.

"Kearney air to Kearney ground. We're at the Minden bridge and beginning our transect," I say into the handheld radio. I'm in the front seat of a three-passenger Cessna 172, next to our pilot, Tom. In the back seat, Lanny notes the time on his clipboard chart. It's thirty minutes before sunrise, and we're 750 feet above the Platte River, looking for whooping cranes.

For the four and a half weeks of fall migration, I'm a part-time employee — a biological technician, no less — of AIM Environmental, a small consulting firm that, since 2000, has conducted monitoring flights along the Platte's Big Bend, contracted first by the U.S. Fish and Wildlife Service and later by the Platte River Recovery Implementation Program. Our job is to spot any whoopers that have roosted overnight on the Platte, fix the precise location of the roost, and then see where the birds fly when they leave the river, so that other technicians can monitor their movements. The purpose of the surveys is to gain more understanding of the habitat characteristics that migrant whooping cranes prefer, for both nighttime roosts and daytime feeding sites.

If we locate whooping cranes this morning, we'll radio their coordinates to one of the spotters on the ground, who will drive along the road just south of the river and watch for the birds to fly over. Then biological technicians, working in shifts, will observe the cranes all day, noting whether they feed in crop fields or wetlands and recording their behavior at fifteen-minute intervals — feeding, resting, alert . . . feeding. One of us will stay within sight of the birds until they either take off to continue their migration or return to the river for the night. Tomorrow morning we'll repeat the process.

We're in the Kearney plane, flying the west transect, from Highway 10 north of Minden to Lexington and back. Meanwhile, another plane takes off from Grand Island and flies the eastern transect between the Minden bridge and Chapman, fifty river miles to the east. In the past few seasons, the west transect has been the dog. Most days, we fly along looking for cranes but wind up mostly looking around and overhearing radio chatter from the other transect: "Three birds near the Wood River bridge. Might be cranes; we're circling for a closer look." Then, "Five white birds at Rowe; we're circling." If I see no cranes today — again — that's all right. My consolation is that I get to see the Platte River from the air, as birds see it.

We bank and cross the Minden bridge, skirting the western end of Rowe Sanctuary. The little Cessna tracks the main channel's south bank as we fly upstream. Lanny and I look down at the streams and sandbars, searching for anything brilliant white. The headsets over our ears block out all sounds but the plane's radio and our three voices. They heighten my sense of seclusion from the rest of the world. It's just the three of us and the river in twilight.

For the first few miles upstream, channels alternately unravel and knit themselves back together, forming sandbars and islands large and small. We fly past the old railroad bridge where I have stood many times and gazed along twisting channels that seem to vanish among the willows and cottonwoods. Hundreds of sandhill cranes roosted there last spring. My view at ground level was of wings fluttering into the darkness between two banks of skeletal trees. From the air, I can see what the cranes liked: the channel broadens at its northward bend, and a patchwork of sandbars lie just beneath the water's surface.

Large sandbars and small islands — the distinction is rather subjective — dwell only part-time under water, but their surfaces generally are bare sand. Larger islands are frizzed with weeds, and a few very large islands are forested. On the largest island, though, is the Speidell Tract, an open expanse of rippled wet meadow, and, in the middle of it, the solitary farmhouse where the Nature Conservancy's land steward lives amid big bluestem, bobwhite quail, grazing cattle, and, each spring, thousands of grazing sandhill cranes. A light shines in the kitchen window. Now we are four. Good morning.

We approach the "Wyoming property" — a tract the State of Wyoming agreed to buy and protect from development as part of a 1987 court settlement regarding the proposed Deer Creek Dam and Reservoir. Here, trees have been cleared; islands and sandbars, kept bare. It's what we describe as "good crane habitat," and indeed, this is one of the spots where whooping cranes have roosted in years past. But not when I was looking.

Upstream and downstream of the Wyoming property, the riverbank and bottomland are thick with trees, and the trees are still thick with leaves. In their shade are a few fine homes, most with decks overlooking, or even overhanging, the water. Sometimes I feel a twinge of envy. Although the river below me is less beautiful than the Platte River of memory, those might still be awfully nice places to live. On the other hand, if the Platte were its old self for one week in late spring, many of these houses would be swamped, and their bird feeders and Adirondack chairs, swept downstream.

I look down at the Meyers Foundation land and across the series of fracturing, sprawling streams. As usual, I start counting channels. Today I get to nine before time runs out; next we're over the Kearney bridge and a single, wide, fast-moving channel.

North of the main channel are quarries like the ones that mark nearly every bridge crossing along the central Platte. Between miniature mountains of gravel and sand are borrow pits filled with groundwater — all connected to the Platte — which percolates in to fill up the empty space that was once filled with sand. Amid the trees and grass, the quarries look blank — like the pale scar left behind when a scab falls away.

The twisted blue rope labeled "Platte River" on most maps bears little resemblance to what we see from the air. The wide valley where the Platte once flowed — rising, dropping, shifting, and sometimes flooding — is now for much of its length a ragged-looking cottonwood forest through which two or more attenuate streams meander as if they had lost their way. In autumn the corridor of forest is mostly a pale, yellowish green — the color of withering leaves — splashed with dark-green clumps of cedar trees. Where the cedars grow thick, the deep, impenetrable green blocks our view of the water. No crane habitat here.

In some stretches, where trees are fewer, cattle graze between the channels. Their worn paths interweave with long, twisted streaks that are the river's footprints. Some are ribbons of pale, dry sand; others are overgrown by weeds but still visible as winding depressions.

Every few miles, we see signs of restoration work — trees removed, sloughs excavated, islands reshaped into sandbars, and water flowing in braided channels. We sit up straight and look down. If we're going to see a whooping crane anywhere, it will almost certainly be on one of these stretches.

Tom, while watching our course, is alert to his passengers'
signals. When Lanny raises his binoculars, Tom asks, "See something?" ready to circle if necessary.

"No. I thought so at first, but those are pelicans," Lanny
answers. If Lanny says pelicans, they're pelicans. Though given
to self-deprecation, Lanny is a crack birder who can identify
species of gulls as they fly past the plane.

At the Lexington bridge, we turn east again. Our return trip
is one of seven randomly chosen transects: we're sometimes one,
two, or three miles north of the river; sometimes right over the
channel; and sometimes to the south. I push the button on my
radio and remind the ground crew that today's return transect
is two miles south of the river.

Heading east, we still look out the windows, although we
have little chance of seeing a crane while most of the corn is
still in the fields. The pale-brown stalks stretch in mile-long
rows that look, from the air, like a giant bristle brush. Here
and there, cattle graze in pastures that are either too wet or
too uneven for a tractor and plow.

Back at the Minden bridge, we bank steeply over the western
part of Rowe Sanctuary and look straight down into the water
at the contours and interwoven colors of the river-bottom sand
and gravel. Sandbars and small islands show themselves as what
they actually are: high spots on an undulating riverbed—some
days inundated, some days not.

The plane levels out, and we head for the airport. In the
cornfields close to the river, a pattern appears through the
bristles: long, indented streaks, where the ground dips in old
channels. No matter how much water humans take from the
river or how much we forget about the Platte's old ways, the land
remembers. The indentations remind me of the chalk rubbings

hobbyists make of tombstones. I imagine spreading a great sheet of paper over the fields and rubbing them with chalk to preserve this channel's epitaph. But of course, it's already saved here for anyone who looks from the vantage point of a crane.

On the way to the airport I look one more time at the river, as I do at the end of each flight. Someday, I'll take my last survey flight, and all of this will become a memory. I look downstream again and think this is the memory that will survive. No whooping cranes, but a silver bundle of ribbons shining in the morning light.

My first views of whooping cranes in Nebraska were mildly disappointing. I can't even find the dates in my journal or field notes. At least twice, Mark and I drove to one Rainwater Basin wetland or another, where cranes had been reported. We parked on the far side of the wetland, a half mile or so away, and fixed the spotting scope on them. The birds — two or three of them — stood at the water's edge, heads tucked under their wings against the chill wind. Maybe their feathers ruffled. Certainly the spotting scope shook in the wind. One of us probably said something like, "So. There they are." We looked. The cranes stood there. The wind blew. We drove home.

More recently, I visited the International Crane Foundation (ICF) during a summer trip to Wisconsin. There, in a small roof-covered amphitheater next to a sheltered wetland, I listened to a talk about ICF's role in crane research, captive breeding, habitat protection, and introduction of an experimental eastern flock of whooping cranes. Meanwhile, a pair of whoopers foraged in the wetland behind our tour leader, apparently undisturbed. Later, after the tour, I wandered back on my own to the front row of the whooping crane exhibit and leaned against a pillar, hoping for a closer look at the cranes and a chance to take photos. Soon, the birds obliged, walking slowly within yards of the shelter. I snapped photo after photo: cranes together, cranes apart, against a bulrush-and-goldenrod background, reflected in the water, heads down, heads up. Later, at home, I reviewed my photos with satisfaction, until I realized my mistake. I had ignored the advice I often give visitors I meet on the Platte: pictures are nice, but they can't take the place of memories. Absorbed in my "great shots," I had failed to really experience the presence of two live whooping cranes when they stood right before me.

I *really saw* whooping cranes one April morning in 2008. I was assigned to monitor a family of cranes—a mated pair and their yearling chick—that had been roosting in a wetland two miles south of the Platte in Gosper County. I drove forty miles in the dark and the rain, feeling resigned—I was probably in for four long hours of watching three birds stand with their heads under their wings. Great. I arrived a bit later than I should have, just at sunrise, and drove slowly along the mud roads, searching. Stopping the car, I scanned the field with my binoculars, east to west, hoping they hadn't flown off before my arrival, wondering how I would explain that I had missed them. I'd be the goat. I'd be . . . wait . . . there! Three bright-white spots appeared above the corn stubble. The birds were surprisingly easy to see, even a half mile away. The brilliant white was not just visible but arresting. Relieved more than excited, I eased the car down the road to a spot with a better view and settled in to watch the backs of three birds with their heads down, feeding.

On the back of my data sheet, I drew a map of the farm—corn stubble here, soybean stubble there, wetland to the south. I had scarcely marked the location of the cranes when, as if to foil me, they spread their wings and glided north for a few dozen yards. Their wings seemed to flow rather than flap, an effortless, casual motion. Flying was simply the easiest way to get from the cornfield to the bean field.

For the sake of consistency, I was supposed to record the behavior of only the juvenile bird. The young bird, not yet a year old, had spent the winter under its parents' vigilant care. It was as large as they were and nearly as white, but with rusty patches on its head that made it easy to distinguish from the adults.

The cranes resumed feeding, and I closed the car window again to keep the rain out. Every fifteen minutes, I partially lowered the window, attached the spotting scope, saw the juvenile feeding while the adults either fed or stood alert, noted "feeding" on my data sheet, closed the widow, and wiped raindrops off my gear. So it went. Feeding, feeding, feeding, feeding. Of course, that's what migrating birds are supposed to do.

Until they don't. Without warning, the parents began to do what male and female cranes are supposed to do. One leapt in the air once and then a second time, its long wings spread and its legs bobbing forward. Soon the pair drifted away from the feeding youngster and alternately leapt, bobbed, and bowed, their wings and long necks in fluid motion. After a minute or two, the dance ended as abruptly as it had begun, and the adults returned to their offspring with a graceful jumble of dancing, skipping, and flying, with their wings outspread, luminous, and flowing.

"Oh!" I heard my own whisper as if it came from someplace else. The cranes stopped, stood alert, and then lowered their heads. Feeding. I closed the window and looked around to see that everything — the spotting scope, the steering wheel, my clothing — was soaked.

Somehow my data sheet was spared, or at least salvageable. A spreadsheet for recording times, locations, and behavior, it was in no way spectacular compared to the sight of a crane's outstretched wings. Yet my hand-drawn map and plodding notes — feeding, feeding, feeding — contribute to one of the conservation measures Robert Porter Allen recommended in his whooping crane monograph: more research. Someday, in an office someplace, a biologist may add these notes to the stacks of data that might help us protect the whooping crane from the greatest threat they face: rampant humanity.

To the extent that we humans have protected whooping cranes from ourselves, their numbers have gradually risen. The 1973 Endangered Species Act was a key element in protecting migration habitat along the Platte River, as Allen had recommended. The 1973 act also paved the way for the U.S. Fish and Wildlife Service's Whooping Crane Recovery Plan, which includes measures Allen could scarcely have envisioned in 1952. The plan, written and regularly revised by a team of wildlife biologists from partner organizations, rests on the foundation that, to be removed from the list of endangered species, whooping cranes must have three geographically separate, self-sustaining wild populations. The existence of separate populations would help shelter the species from shocks like the Texas drought that decimated the cranes' food staple, blue crabs, in the winter of 2008–9, contributing to the death of twenty-three birds, nearly 10 percent of the flock.

The effort to build independent populations, starting from zero, has included white-costumed biologists teaching captive-raised chicks to feed and fly; leg bands fitted with radio transmitters to track hand-reared birds; and ultralight aircraft leading young birds on their first migration.

Here in Nebraska, my data collection seems quaint by comparison, but it suits me well enough — making scratch marks on paper by the flickering light of white wings.

In late October I drive to Mormon Island for a visit with Karine Gil, a population ecologist at the Crane Trust. A native of Venezuela, Karine earned her PhD at Texas A & M University, where her research on crane migration began.

The sky is gray, the grass along Wild Rose Drive is rusty brown, and the air feels damp and chilly as I trot from my car toward the trust's headquarters building, but within Karine's office all is light and cheery. Photos of whooping cranes, sandhill cranes, and the Platte River cover her walls, her desk, and her filing cabinet. She has photos of fellow ornithologists, crane memorabilia. Tiny whooping crane earrings peek out from the thick brown hair that frames her broad, animated face. Karine is a five-foot dynamo. And she doesn't just study cranes; she lives and breathes cranes. I prepare to sit across from her at her desk and pull out my notebook, but Karine has other ideas. She beckons me over to her computer, which displays an interactive map of the central plains states, showing red and blue dots where whoopers were sighted on this year's migration. The dots are more concentrated in central Nebraska than elsewhere, but still, there aren't many dots at all. "So, it looks like most whooping cranes get all the way from Wood Buffalo to Aransas without anyone seeing them," I offer.

Karine nods. "Or maybe people see them but don't report them," she says, and scrolls the map northward, across the Niobrara River, through South Dakota. "And do we have more sightings in Nebraska because more cranes stop here or because more people are looking? These are some of the things we don't know. Now. Look at this." She switches to another map with more dots and then toggles over to a spreadsheet. I have trouble keeping up.

If Karine talks fast, maybe it's because she's in a race against time. The key to conserving migration habitat in the face of tight budgets and accelerating energy development — particularly wind farm development — is to pinpoint and then protect the most important areas. But to do that, she says, "we need to know *where* the cranes go and *why*. We need more data to do the science."

The potential effects of wind turbines on whooping cranes are still being debated. What *is* known is that other species of birds — including significant numbers of raptors — have been killed by collisions with wind turbines. Migrating cranes fly far above the height of a turbine. However, during stopovers, they make low-altitude flights back and forth between roosts and feeding sites. Apart from whatever danger turbines them-selves may or may not pose to cranes, power lines are a certain hazard. And where there are wind farms, there are power lines. Biologists also know that whooping cranes often avoid areas that contain anything the birds perceive as a disturbance. If too much of the cranes' preferred migration habitat is lost to disturbances, they may make fewer stopovers, to the detriment of their health.

On my previous visit, Karine told me about data she had been analyzing from whooping cranes that had been captured and banded at Wood Buffalo National Park in the 1970s and '80s. The color-coded leg bands made it possible, over the years, for observers to distinguish the otherwise-indistinguishable birds and make inferences regarding pair bonds, family groups, and behaviors — including migration behavior. In particular, based on her analysis, Karine is convinced that whooping cranes exhibit site fidelity during migration. In other words, individual birds and family groups visit the same migration stopovers repeatedly in their lifetimes and even appear to transmit their "traditions" to succeeding generations. If she's right, site fidelity is a powerful argument for protecting known migration habitat — the sort of argument that could tell, say, a wind farm developer, "Build it *there*, not *here*."

Karine's data have come from a dwindling number of birds. Only 133 were banded in the first place, and the few that survive are near, or even beyond, their twenty- to thirty-year expected life span. She tells me research will make a great leap forward with results of a new project to band another generation of whooping cranes, using bands fitted with GPS transmitters.

But Karine can't wait for that. She's hustling around her tiny office gathering up the gear we'll need to drive a Whooper Watch route. Into the tote bag go binoculars, spotting scope, camera, and a folder of flyers and data sheets. Karine has recruited and trained a group of local volunteers for the Whooper Watch program. They drive prescribed routes during migration seasons and report any whooping cranes they spot, so that movements, feeding patterns, and behavior can be monitored. She also carries the hotline cell phone, whose number she has advertised in press releases and posted in public places all around the Big Bend region.

"Here." She holds out a handful of cellophane packages to me. "You can put one of these in your car and give the others to friends." The packages hold circular cardboard air fresheners, each on an elastic band for attachment to a rearview mirror. I take a sniff — apple. The discs feature a drawing of a whooping crane and the toll-free hotline number. Now if I see a whooping crane on my way home, the next thing I'll see is the 800 number, so that I can notify Whooper Watch.

We climb into Karine's SUV and head west to drive the dirt roads south of the Platte. Although she has a team of volunteers driving their respective routes, Karine is not the type to sit at her desk waiting for the phone to ring. She drives a route daily during the migration.

The corn is still standing in many fields — no place for cranes there — but when we reach a pasture, bean field, or harvested cornfield, we scan for big white birds. In Buffalo County, where the road bends close to the river, Karine pulls over to photograph a channel where cranes lately roosted. Several sandbars peek out of the water, which is low today; across the channel is an island covered in phragmites. Not ideal crane habitat, but apparently it was good enough.

We drive south out of the river valley to a field where a family group recently spent the day feeding. While Karine hops out to take photos of the pasture, I pull the folder from her tote bag and rifle through the papers. She has several fliers to explain the Whooper Watch program, and others with drawings that show how to distinguish a whooping crane from sandhills, pelicans, snow geese, and egrets. With these papers, she's ready to recruit new volunteers if she strikes up a conversation with curious passersby. She also carries small orange Whooper Watch posters to tack up in gas stations and cafés wherever she goes. The poster gives the hotline number and explains, "When reports are made, Whooper Watch sends scientists out to monitor the whooping cranes so they can learn more about what these birds need to survive."

Karine drives and scans; I scan and steal glances at the map I've pulled from her folder. The spots of recent crane sightings are marked with *X*s. I guess at the routes of the other drivers. All those eyes, looking for cranes, looking especially hard in places marked with an *X*. The approach seems, not exactly methodical, but thoroughgoing: a community of people searching every haystack and overturning every stone.

On the way back to the Crane Trust, we talk about some of the sites where cranes have been spotted more than once. Because most birds are unbanded, there's no proof the same birds are making repeat visits. For now, Karine focuses on site characteristics — what makes migrating cranes choose a certain spot, and will they keep coming back? "I don't know if whooping cranes *think*," she says, "but they definitely have memory."

In a week, autumn crane surveys will be just a memory, and still I've seen no whooping cranes on our transect. I did hear the talk, though, about a group of seven cranes that the east crew are monitoring in Hall County. So I phoned and left a message with Gary Lingle, the program coordinator, to ask if I could take a turn.

"You know where they are, don't you?" he asked, when he called back in the morning. (One of Gary's appealing qualities is that he treats me as if I knew more than I really do.) He named a farm owner who manages his stretch of the river for crane habitat and who gives our group permission to monitor the whoopers that regularly visit. Another biotech, Chuck, was scheduled to watch the birds this morning and can only stay until noon. "But if I were you, I'd get there before ten," Gary said. "We've got a north wind, and those guys are ready to go."

It feels warm for early November — fifty-five degrees maybe — and the sky is solid blue with the faintest wisps of clouds on the horizon. I drive through an open gate, past a sign that reads, "No Trespassing," and ease the tires through puddled water, following the directions Chuck gave me when I phoned him . . . where the path bends right by the trees, follow the tracks straight ahead. Are these tracks? I hesitate and then see a vehicle ahead; I inch across the mowed meadow, between the corn and the river and among a scattering of huge round bales, bumping through swales and ridges softened only slightly by grass, to the spot where Chuck is parked. He motions for me to pull up alongside his car. Wherever the birds may be, I apparently needn't have worried about disturbing them, because Chuck, a tall, round-headed, square-shouldered man in his seventies, is out walking around. I get out, wondering where the cranes are and hoping this guy knows what he's doing. Chuck points to the northeast, across the water toward a large, weedy sandbar, just visible above the clustered shrubs on the bank. Way over there? Through binoculars, I can pick out seven birds near the sandbar's edge and see them just well enough to discern that some have their heads up, others down, feeding. Leftmost is the cinnamon-tinged juvenile bird — the one we monitor. Chuck walks me around to the driver's side of his car, where his spotting scope is set up, and I get a clearer view — good enough to really see what the birds are doing.

We get in his car to look at his data sheet, which begins at 7:45. He tells me that for most of the morning, the juvenile has been in the middle of the flock, flanked by three adults on each side. He checks his watch — 8:30 — gets out, looks through the scope, and returns. "Resting," he says, as if thinking aloud. "It was feeding before." He makes a few notes and then looks up at me. "So. Who is it you're with, again?"

I tell him that I write part-time for the Rainwater Basin Joint Venture and that I'm also writing a book about the Platte River that springs in part from my volunteer work at Rowe Sanctuary.

"We probably know some of the same people," he says. "I retired from the Fish and Wildlife Service in Grand Island." So he does know what he's doing, I think. But that's just the beginning of the story. Chuck first came to Grand Island in the 1960s. An early assignment, he tells me, was to review and reapprove the Fish and Wildlife Service's official opinion paper on the pending Mid-State Reclamation Project. In his judgment, the report was badly flawed and seriously understated the Platte River's importance as crane habitat. But he felt he needed data — and a degree — to back up his argument. "So I took a leave of absence and went to Kearney State for my master's degree," he says.

As he talks, my mind races: Chuck ... Charles ... the survey schedules list only first names, so I'd never paid much attention to who ... He pauses and, apologizing, I interrupt: "Charles Frith. The sandhill crane study. I read your thesis." He nods.

After earning his degree, Chuck worked briefly in Colorado and then in Omaha before returning to the Fish and Wildlife Service in Grand Island. Back on the Platte, he helped to write the Fish and Wildlife Service's *Platte River Ecology Study*, a first-of-its-kind research report, published in 1981, that guided early conservation work along the river. For the rest of his years with the service, he was deeply involved in Platte River issues. After retirement, he worked part-time for the National Audubon Society as a consultant, assisting NAS's efforts to protect the Platte.

Chuck doesn't brag, just tells me what happened. "Anyway," he says, "since you're writing about the river, I thought you'd want to know about that." He looks at his watch and gets out to check the spotting scope. We agree to talk again later and shake hands. He gives me the data sheet, and I say, "Thanks ...," but for much more than the sheet of paper. "For what you did, I mean, and for telling me."

When Chuck drives away, I pull my Subaru into his spot and start the process of adjusting my window to the best height, attaching my spotting scope on the window mount, adjusting, readjusting, cursing mildly when my aim is off. Finally, I decide the best arrangement is to keep the car door open, with the window nearly closed and the scope squeezed into the gap. I'm looking through the scope and adjusting the focus knob when everything suddenly blurs. I reverse the knob, but no, it's not the focus. The white-and-black blur vanishes from the frame. What's this? I look up and see the birds — just white spots — in motion, some in flight. I raise my binoculars in time to see the last two birds take a few steps and then rise up, their wings sweeping the air. They fly west and then briefly north, gaining altitude; I fear that they'll fly away and that I'll be the spotter who lost sight of the cranes. But as my heart starts to pound, they bank east and then south across the channel, looking larger and larger as they approach me, flying in single file. Their flight seems slow, almost leisurely compared to that of sandhill cranes; so I have a few seconds to alternately hope and dread that they will fly right over me. Do I duck into the car so as not to frighten them? Or stand stock-still? The cranes answer by shifting their course slightly so that when they fly past, the car is between us, with just my head above the roof. Perhaps they are not afraid of me. "Relax," says the voice in my head. "Just look — hard. You may never see this again." I lean against the car and look with all my being. The flock circles twice and emerges in a sharp V formation, with the golden-colored juvenile in second position. The other birds are beyond white; they are luminous. Sun strikes the dazzling feathers, shines through them perhaps. The black wing tips only amplify the white brilliance. They call in voices high-pitched and hollow, and I try to record it in my mind but know it's impossible. The cranes' wings rise and fall in liquid motion, pure black, pure white, on a pure-blue sky. To my right, the cranes bank and the V points south. They cross the field, cross the treetops, and leave me blinking the black spots from my sunstruck eyes.

On the morning of the final whooping crane survey flight, I am the ground crew, which means I sit in my car beside the bridge south of Overton and listen for radio transmissions from the survey plane. I'm supposed to be ready to track any cranes the surveyors spot, though I've never yet been called to do that, so mostly I look around and think.

The sun is just beginning to rise. A hot orange pink bubbles up from the eastern horizon, and sunrise shines pearly blue white through the tops of heaped-up blue clouds. Above me, high, thin clouds flow eastward, fast and steady, like a river.

And in the west, the moon shines golden behind the nearly bare cottonwood branches, a glowing light behind low clouds. As I watch, it slides lower and appears below the clouds, a bright coin dropping toward the horizon. The radio crackles, "Kearney air to Kearney ground." The survey plane passes over, heading west, a red light blinking aft, green light fore, and a white flashing light on each wing. Strange. It feels sturdy enough when I'm inside it, but from this vantage point the Cessna looks frail, like a tiny ship in a vast sea.

A few minutes later I hear Lanny's voice on the radio as the plane turns and starts its return transect two miles north of the river. That's my cue to start driving back to Kearney. I'll give them a few minutes to overtake me and then head east, tracking the plane's return route.

I drive south to the first road that parallels the river. At the stop sign, I look across land that is flat, flat as calm water, for as far as I can see. A little farmstead and hay bales in the distance are wrapped in pink mist. The clouds, also pink, are shredding apart in the sunlight.

I scan the sky as I drive, knowing I am unlikely to see a whooping crane. Throughout the migration, Gary sends weekly updates to the surveyors, telling us how many cranes have been spotted along the migration route and at Aransas. So I know that by now most, if not all, of the birds have passed the Platte. At the end of each email, Gary signs off with, "Keep your eyes to the sky!" As if we could stop. Weeks from now, I'll still be looking.

Window open, I drive along slowly, listening for birds. I still feel slightly elated after my encounter a few days ago with the seven cranes. Their sunlit white shines in my memory, and I feel as if I had been handed a membership card to an exclusive club.

Idly I turn the numbers over in my head. Seven. What percentage is that of all the whooping cranes in the world? Or of the Aransas–Wood Buffalo flock? In truth, I stopped keeping track of whooping crane statistics after 2008. Before then, I could add a few numbers each year and make a close guess; subtraction complicates the arithmetic and clouds the memory.

Something—like a cold stone—turns over in my stomach. It is a privilege to be part of an exclusive club, but lifetime membership carries a lifetime burden. It brings the risk of joining an even smaller society of people: those who recall the sight and sound of a species after the last of its kind has died.

I'm still driving, watching the sky, the tree line along the river, and the fields of corn stubble. If it's too soon to call whooping crane conservation a success story, it is also too soon to despair. Still, I suspect that if whooping cranes ceased to be, I would consider the people born too late to be more fortunate than I. Fortunate that they would not forever feel compelled to scan the sky and look across each field, endlessly searching the emptiness.

8 *Outside Home*

LATE NOVEMBER

The corn harvest in the central Platte valley is winding down. At the Buffalo County Fairgrounds near my house and at crossroads and rail spurs around the region, golden mountains of corn kernels have piled higher and higher for weeks, while vistas grow ever broader above the miles of shorn brown cornstalks. The constant rumble-whine of combines has faded, and instead I hear sparrows as I run along the path at the Fort Kearny State Recreation Area.

This is a path I know by heart. A path I initially hated. I hated almost everything when we first moved to Kearney. Unmoored and endlessly sad in this foreign landscape, I sought the only cure that had worked for me in the past — long runs, and lots of them. But where to run? Kearney's so-called hike-bike trail was concrete paved, like most of the city, and made my knees almost as sore as my heart.

Of the two dirt paths I found near Kearney, Cottonmill Park's two-mile loop was the one I wanted to like. Up and down through sand prairie hills with yuccas and tallgrass, it was challenging and varied. But the view from the hilltop was of earthmoving equipment and of five-thousand-square-foot houses abuilding all around the park's perimeter. The sound of power hammers and rumbling excavators followed me around the loop and only deepened my despair.

So I kept returning to the path I fairly hated — the state park's converted rail bed. It was dead flat and dead straight, skirting cornfield and quarry, one end in the shadow of I-80. At least it crossed the river. Back and forth I ran, a paltry 1.8 miles each way. Out. Back. Even a short run meant I had to see everything twice. Long runs meant mind-numbing repetition. Mind-numbing, that is, until I started to notice things — things like the opening by the bridge where deer always cross the trail; the woodpile where magpies often perch; the patch of penstemons blooming purple and pink; a school of minnows in shallow water, all facing upstream, their tiny shadows wiggling on the sandy riverbed.

A few months after our move, I trained for a marathon on the path that I was beginning merely to dislike. Back and forth I ran — five circuits, six circuits, seven. I kept track of round-trips with a pile of pebbles at the south turnaround. At the end of every circuit, I transferred one pebble from the left pile to the right.

In late winter the migration began. For the first time in my life, I heard flocks of snow geese approaching before they were visible — flocks so huge they sounded like giant, roaring engines. The geese were a welcome distraction, because the wind and sleet blew so hard some days that I had to stop and turn my back to catch my breath. Soon cranes began to arrive, skimming over my head toward the cornfield. The path thawed and squished beneath my feet.

Weeks later, springtime birds sang as if to introduce themselves when they arrived: eastern phoebes, brown thrashers, towhees, Baltimore and orchard orioles. Hello. Hello. Bird food arrived, too — insects, including gnats that I inhaled and swallowed. In May, tractors drove back and forth in the fields, planting evenly spaced rows of corn, straight as the path. And I ran, back and forth.

After the marathon, I continued to run on the path, not minding it too much anymore and wanting to see what happened next. To avoid the summer heat, I often ran at twilight. Running past the open meadow in June, I watched while thunderheads massed over Phelps County in the sunset's glow. As the clouds rolled closer, pulsing with lightning flashes, I calculated whether I could outrun their approach and finish one more circuit.

The nights calmed in midsummer, and fireflies came out in the river bottoms beneath the bridge. I looked down, not on dozens or hundreds, but on tens of thousands of twinkling fireflies. It was like gazing down on city lights from the Empire State Building or like Fourth of July fireworks over Lake Michigan. Or like a star-filled sky in rural Nebraska.

On daytime runs, I tracked the progress of the straight rows of corn growing taller, forming tassels. That year, the river ran dry in late summer. Purple loosestrife and phragmites hastened their march along the banks and islands; in between, the dry channels showed ripples and long streaks, as if some prankster had used sand to draw a picture of flowing water.

When actual water showed up in October, waterfowl showed up, too: cackling geese, mallards, northern shovelers. Many were on their way to their wintering grounds, as were the small flocks of sandhill cranes that flew over. The cranes didn't land, but sometimes they circled briefly and bugled before resuming their southward flight.

Combines churned back and forth in November, gobbling up full ears of corn and pouring golden streams of kernels into wagons alongside. As a combine harvested the cornfield east of the path, I ran a parallel course and realized I liked some things about this place.

Now another harvest has ended, and I am laying down yet another line of footprints on the path, another thin layer of history. Liquid-sweet birdsong rises from the brambles beside the path — one clear whistle, "*twee-ee-ee*." The Harris's sparrows are stopping here en route to wintering grounds on the southern plains. A second song joins in, similar in nature to the Harris's one-pitch song but buzzier and with rising notes. That's the white-crowned sparrow, also a migrating visitor.

Around here, you can measure the seasons in sparrows. When winter deepens and the white-crowned and Harris's sparrows continue southward, I'll run to the sound of tinkling bells — the calls of American tree sparrows huddled in brush piles and bare-twigged shrubs at the woodland edges. January's first hints of spring will include northbound white-crowned and Harris's sparrows, singing here again after a short absence. In mid-March, with the influx of sandhill cranes will come song sparrows, singing their lively tune from the willows beneath the bridge. Later in the spring, grasshopper sparrows will arrive and begin to trill in the tallgrass meadows; next, field sparrows will sing their bouncing song and continue to sing all summer. One day I will realize that I haven't heard a field sparrow for a while, that farmers are pulling and stacking their irrigation pipes, and that I have grown another year older. Soon after, I'll hear the Harris's sparrow again.

Tomorrow's forecast calls for snow, but today it is shirt-sleeve weather. The sky is smooth blue, a glass bowl, and the midday sun behind me casts my shadow on the bridge. In a month the sun's course will reach its lowest angle in our sky and will then, we trust, repeat its circuit.

The shining bowl above me calls to mind the lodges in which Pawnee villagers dwelt in centuries past, when they lived along the Platte and its tributaries. An earth lodge's shape echoed the dome of the sky, and through the smoke hole at its apex, the stars were visible at night. The seasonal course of the stars across the night sky, along with specific weather changes and the position of the sun, guided the Pawnees' annual cycle of ceremonies, work, and migration — traditions shaped by the landscape in which they dwelt.

At this time of year, the Pawnees were on the move. Their summer crops harvested and stored, they departed their villages in the weeks that we call late October and early November for the winter buffalo hunt. They crossed the Platte and followed an age-old path along the south bank, traveling westward and finally south. In a landscape that to pioneers seemed feature- less, the people who knew it best saw landmarks that guided their way.

As I run along, I watch the ground, considering the sounds my feet make and wondering idly whether I could recognize my whereabouts on this path by sound alone. The hollow wooden sound of the trestle bridge — that's easy. But does black earth sound different than sand? I'd know the Speidell Tract entrance because noisy bobwhites often hide in a nearby shrub. I could find each wetland in the spring and summer according to which frogs were singing. And of course, in the spring and fall I would recognize the quarter-mile mark at the path's south end by the whistling "*twee-ee-ee*" of far-ranging sparrows that, twice a year, find their way back to one precise twenty-foot patch of brambles.

A chorus of squeaks and yelps overhead interrupts my reverie. I look up at a hundred snow geese heading south. It's a late flock, maybe the last I'll see this year. About half the birds are snowy white, almost silver in the slanting sunlight. The rest are blue geese — the darker members of their species, slate colored and white with all-white heads. In a sense, these birds are newcomers, like me. Old-timers along the Mississippi River flyway recall when migrating snow geese were plentiful there. Migration-range maps from the 1970s show snow geese migrating through Iowa and along the Missouri River, but gradually the snow goose migration has shifted west. At this latitude the change is noticeable in the fall but is much more dramatic in the spring, when the millions of birds are concentrated into a region just a few hundred miles wide, where they threaten to crowd out other species.

Apparently, as land uses and other conditions changed across the Midwest, snow geese relocated to surroundings in which they were more likely to thrive. That's not so different from what our human ancestors have done for millennia. Instead of funneling into a small area, though, emigrating humans have spread out, flooding over the planet's surface and displacing — or extirpating — previous inhabitants, both human and nonhuman.

My own ancestors were part of the deluge. The first wave washed ashore on the rocky North Atlantic coast; the other side of the family swept across the continent to California's Imperial Valley. And so now, we call this continent home.

But which of us can name the night stars above our heads

and correlate their movements with the changing seasons? I have never even thought to try.

All my life, I have lived like an exile, even in the place where I grew up. Movements of the stars and sun, migratory birds, my Native predecessors? I didn't even know which way the nearest river flowed.

I am hardly unique. We are a people whose histories trail behind us, across continents and oceans. But in the present, we find that we can live just fine — prosper even — without the local knowledge and the visceral connection to the earth that were once essential, not just for physical survival, but for spiritual sustenance.

In the future, though — for the sake of the future — I would like to change. If the future brings a disrupted climate, water shortages, displaced wildlife, more frequent petroleum accidents, and a host of other environmental ills, they will have been caused at least in part by our failure to understand the ground on which we live. If I am to help fix what is broken, maybe I should start by doing my homework.

Besides, I am ready to stop living like an exile. The problem remains, though, that I cannot point to any single place and call it "home." The home of my ancestors? Which ones? The path backward has so many forks, intersections, and unmarked passages — it seems impossible to trace. I could wind up on England's North Devon Coast, on a hillside in Switzerland, or in some unmapped harbor in northern Labrador. As for the place where I was born, the places of my earliest memories, first apartment, first house — all are somebody else's home, not mine.

For many years, I have felt nostalgia for something I can't

name — a tug toward some place that, if I found it, might be the center of everything. I'm no longer sure that place exists.

My best hope may be to grab a likely handhold — the familiar feel of a trestle bridge beneath my feet or a twenty-foot patch of brambles and the sweet-rich whistle of sparrows that always find their way back to this very spot.

9   *This Living Planet*

DECEMBER

Dusk. Vision folds in on itself as daylight drains away. In the pale southwest sky, small clumps of plum-colored clouds trail faint streaks, as though a great hand had dragged them across the heavens. The horizon, tinted pink, peeks through a fringe of naked branches. Twenty honking, squeaking geese glide in a black chevron toward the sinking sun, to the slough upstream where they'll roost tonight.

Winter's first snowfall dusted the Platte valley two weeks ago but has long since melted. Now, like melted snow, all the colors of late summer and fall are seeping into the ground as well. Corn that grew six feet tall and vibrant green has been lopped into rows of foot-tall stalks, crisp and tan in furrowed gray-brown soil.

In the former cornfield on my right, now a restored meadow, the corn's wild kin have faded as well. Cordgrass, wild ryes, Indian grass, and bluestems, once in shades of summer greens and purples, now are rusty gold. Once-plump seed heads have ripened and scattered across the meadow to await April's rain;

they left behind bare, spiky stalks that rattle softly in the breeze. The grasses look nearly lifeless, and above the ground, they are. But below the surface, the network of roots, six feet deep, will stay alive throughout the winter and through countless winters to come, growing thicker and more intertwined as the years pass, perhaps someday to match the thickly woven web of life that formed native prairie sod.

The last few brown leaves that cling doggedly to the cottonwood trees crackle above my head. From most of the trees and shrubs along the river, all the leaves have fallen and blown away, exposing gray branches and, among them, abandoned birds' nests, large and small. I pause by a dogwood and peer inside a nest. It's dead looking, brown, gray, and black, but once held tiny living eggs. The young birds that hatched and fledged from most nests along this path — the fortunate ones, at least — have flown south to warmer latitudes where insects fly and seeds will not be covered by snow. But in the spring, many will find their way back here — to the place where they first saw the sky — to build nests of their own and repeat the cycle of life.

I am thinking this evening of my son, who is nearly grown and ready to start a life of his own. We've taken few walks together by this river, far fewer than suited my vision of the kind of mother I had hoped to be. I can't blame him for disliking the feel of the grasshoppers that clung to our legs in the fall or for his impatience with a mother who wants to stop every few yards to examine flowers, butterflies, and pebbles. I do blame myself sometimes. Graduate school and motherhood don't really mix; maybe I could have done a better job of sharing my fascinations — the sights, sounds, and ideas that, to me, give life meaning. I worry he'll remember instead that I spent his high school years away at the river or away inside a book.

For the past few weeks, though, we were together more than usual. Required as part of his high school curriculum to perform community service, he surprised me by choosing fieldwork at Rowe Sanctuary. Together we walked the sanctuary's bottom-land trails, clearing fallen saplings and low-hanging branches; we chopped cedar trees from the fence line beside the bluebird trail. One day I even coaxed him into a pair of borrowed waders, and we slogged through thigh-deep water, skidding on submerged ice, to pull weeds on one of the tern-and-plover islands. I don't think he loved any of it. But he outworked me; he saw eagles and deer and left his own mark there. And now he knows a part of the world that I inhabit.

At the edge of the meadow, the shadows look strangely dense and dark — and one shadow moves. Through binoculars, I make out ten deer, tawny brown with white throats. Ten black noses point toward me; twenty black-rimmed ears stand alert. I shift my feet just slightly, and half the deer bound away, their white tails flagging an alarm. The others take a few slow steps and are swallowed up in the tall grass.

It's possible that one of those deer is an old acquaintance of mine. We met a year ago in August near this very spot. Out for a short run, I heard twigs snapping and spied a galloping fawn, obviously spooked by the sound of my footsteps. It crashed through the brush, running parallel to my path. The fawn outran me easily and leapt across the path, far ahead of me into the meadow. Or so I assumed.

A few minutes later I heard a pitiful, lamblike bleating. Then, passing a clump of cedars that had blocked my view, I saw its source: the fawn, having failed to leap between the top two strands of a barbed-wire fence, had become entangled. The little animal was suspended by its hips, its front hooves barely touching the ground and one hind leg pinched in the wires beneath it. I walked closer and inspected the nearly hopeless predicament. Then I looked across the field to the nearest farmhouse and silently ticked off a list of people I knew nearby. At midday they would all be away at work; the fawn and I were on our own.

I tried rationally to weigh the costs and benefits. There would be blood — most likely mine. The fawn, like most of its species, might have a short life in any case. It might starve or be hit by a car or wind up in one of my friends' freezers. But any of those deaths would be preferable to what awaited a trapped deer in coyote habitat. And I was responsible. I could have walked away from the fawn but not from the memory of it hanging there, bawling.

Taking a deep breath, I examined the wires, trying and failing to mentally untangle them. Then I grabbed the hind legs, one in each hand. They felt surprisingly tiny — scarcely more than twigs — but their kicks jolted right up to my shoulders. The fawn bleated and flailed in terror as I transferred both kicking legs to my right hand and fought to hold on long enough to push the twisted wires down with my left hand and lift the fawn free. Or something like that. Really, the struggle was too brief and haphazard for me to know what happened, except that just as the fawn's legs slipped from my grasp and it leapt away, I heard a *zing* and knew what that meant. A thin red line blossomed on my wrist and then welled into a bright band.

Clamping my left hand over what I preferred not to see, I strode three-quarters of a mile to my car and steered up Second Avenue with my fingertips and knees to the medical clinic. The bleeding seemed modest — no big drips — and I knew that it could have been much worse. But instead of feeling appalled at the serious damage I might easily have done to myself, I felt slightly exalted by the memory of the fawn's kicking legs. That memory, the feel of it, resides still in my arms and shoulders: the fierce strength of a life bent on survival and my own muscles' answer.

The bemused but kind doctor who stitched my wrist told me not to worry about scarring; with a daily slathering of vitamin E oil, my mishap should leave no trace. I used the vitamin E and didn't worry, and he was almost right. The faint white line blends with the creases at my wrist and is invisible to everyone but me. And I regard it not as a scar but as a memento.

I raise my binoculars again and scan the grass, but the deer have vanished. At the bridge, I take the stairs down to the island. The sand between the dead grasses and thatch is loose and soft; it shifts beneath my feet. Downstream, the pale-gold undersides of two vast wings catch the last rays of sunlight as a great horned owl flies the length of the island and then swoops upward to perch at the top of a gnarled Russian olive tree. Everything on this island may look and feel dead to me, but the owl knows better. Somewhere beneath the thatch, something will eventually move, and although my dull senses might miss it, the owl will see or hear.

At the water's edge, the sand is hard, frozen into a miniature dune field. The ripples, swirls, and waves were formed in the image of the flowing water that created them. Paper-thin ice crackles across the sand as I squat and trail my fingers through water that will freeze tonight, if only for a few hours. It's cold but not painful, and the sandy bottom is pleasingly soft.

I lift my gaze to the white crescent moon in the south sky; just below it are two bright gems of light: Jupiter and Venus on an unusually close rendezvous. Looking out into the universe,

I sense the currents of life that flow about me on this singular planet. Our beautiful but lonely neighbors share the light and warmth of our sun and are made of elements common to us, yet no eyes gaze out from those places to wonder at the blue, watery planet we call Earth.

I suppose this is what I hope to give Andrew on our rare walks together — the solace of knowing that we are made of this planet and are part of its life, as surely as we are part of the lives of our own mothers. We can see life all around us if only we look; we can feel it with our hands and the soles of our feet.

The river gurgles as it laps the sandbars. Its voice proclaims life as insistently as a beating heart. On the brink of winter, that life seems subdued, but in the treetops, beneath the thatch, and deep underground, it persists. I stand, stretch my legs, wipe my cold fingers on the leg of my pants, and start for home.

10 *Teaching Ourselves to See*

JANUARY

Along the Platte River, some of us mark the new year by counting eagles. John Murphy and I are in his SUV, driving west at fifty miles an hour on the smooth blacktop road that runs roughly parallel to the Platte. The river itself, of course, is out of sight, concealed by a corridor of tall cottonwood trees — eagle perches.

In the Jeep behind us are Carol Hines and her brother Jim, who is visiting for the holidays. This is Eagle Watch, an annual tradition of the Audubon Society's local chapter. Big Bend Audubon's membership has waned since its glory days in the 1970s and '80s, when chapters organized to protect the Platte River against Mid-State and other water development projects. But the group's members — which still include a few founders — remain devotees of the Platte and its wildlife.

This year, only a handful of eagle watchers turned up at the rendezvous beside a giant sandhill crane sculpture in the parking lot of the Kearney Chamber of Commerce. We sorted ourselves into three vehicles, and the third car set out for Harlan

Reservoir and the Republican River, its occupants cheerfully determined to outcount us.

Our group's route is a thirty-five-mile stretch of the Platte's Big Bend, where dozens of bald eagles spend the winter. By day many of the birds perch in tall trees along the river, keeping watch over unfrozen areas that might render a meal. Even in cold weather, sloughs and channels fed by groundwater remain above freezing temperature. The largest area of open water, though, will be at our destination, the Johnson-2 hydroelectric plant south of Lexington.

I ask John about the purpose for the annual Eagle Watch, because it's not entirely clear to me — do we keep records or send the data somewhere, as in a Christmas bird count? John, who has been counting eagles for a decade, is not sure either and seems unconcerned. "I think it's mostly social," he says with a shrug, and that sounds like reason enough to me. Besides, I come from a region where "counting eagles" would mean counting to one. If there's a *quantity* of eagles around, who could resist counting?

John, on the other hand, is a Nebraskan. He grew up in Kearney and then moved away to one of those places with sunshine and beaches, as young midwesterners often do. Then, as midwesterners also do, he eventually moved back and found that "home" held its own wonders — like hundreds of bald eagles each winter hiding in plain sight.

I am glad to be riding with John. We've led many Rowe Sanctuary tours together during the crane migration but seldom have a chance to simply go birdwatching. A teacher by profession and by nature, John is respected at Rowe as a knowledgeable and generous guide and the ideal coach for new birdwatchers. He often sets up his spotting scope at the back window in the

Nicolson Center or in a blind and points out some interesting bird. "The focus is on the top," he says, encouraging others to look. If someone calls him over to consult about a discovery — "I think it's a white-throated sparrow," a novice might say — he ambles over to see and commends them, "Yes, indeed." What I admire is his humility. At sunset in an observation blind, he knows it's the cranes that belong in the limelight. "I'll just be quiet now and let you listen to the birds," he sometimes says.

It's a frigid morning, but at least the wind is calm. Several days of sunshine have melted the snow and ice from the road, so John can concentrate less on driving and more on scanning treetops, as I am doing.

"Over there," I say and point to a dark mass in an otherwise undifferentiated rampart of gray trees.

"Yes, indeed." John pulls up sharply on the shoulder so that we can both raise our binoculars. "Looks like a second-year bird," he says, noting its dark head and mottled breast. I concur, and we take off again, with Carol's Jeep in pursuit. At the next stop, we'll find out whether Carol and Jim have seen the same birds or maybe others we have missed.

As I continue to scan the treetops, I wonder aloud if we shouldn't record our observations; in answer John reaches back with his right hand to rummage on the floorboards, eventually producing a small, slightly crushed notebook. I pull a pen from my coat pocket and start the tally.

"There's an adult," one or the other of us says. Or less often, we spot a bird that is heavily streaked brown and white and looks somewhat moth-eaten. "Juvenile," one of us says, and I record it. We stop once on the shoulder, and John sets up the tripod and scope to check a distant bird that might be a hawk . . . or a young eagle. Eagle, the four of us agree. We compare notes with Carol and Jim about birds we have passed, and then we carry on.

The next several birds we record without slowing down. We point and nod; I write. Adults, with their bright-white heads and tails, are easy to spot even at high speed.

Easy to spot. Not for everybody, I suppose. A few years ago, on a long drive across eastern Canada, I apparently perplexed my mother with my habit of pointing out roadside birds. Herons and loons in wetlands. Red-tailed hawks on fence posts and signs. And every few hours, another eagle.

Finally, in New Brunswick, when I said, "bald eagle," and pointed across the St. John River to a dark spot on a far-off tree, she asked, "How do you *do* that?" I couldn't say.

Now, watching John, who is watching the trees even while watching the road, I start to see the answer forming. The secret, partly, is practice — learning the shapes of birds and other wildlife — and partly it's a matter of showing up at the right place. But most importantly, some people are, either by training or by nature, always studying a dark mass in bare treetops, always looking for a flitting movement in the roadside grass, or glancing twice wherever there is water.

Once or twice each minute, one of us spots an eagle, and I make a hash mark in the notebook, in either the adult column or the subadult column. After a few miles, without a word, John turns north, toward the river. No explanation is needed; we're on our way to a vantage point for an eagle's nest that is well-known to local birders. Carol, too, will know where we are going. "We'll just see if anything's happening here," John says. Carol and Jim join us just in time to see a great blue heron launch itself from beneath the bridge. It skims across an expanse of open water and flaps languidly upstream, probably to wait out our intrusion. While John sets up his spotting scope, I raise my binoculars toward the massive nest, a tangled pile of sticks and branches nestled in the fork of a great cottonwood tree. And perched near the end of the forking branch above the river is an adult eagle. We take turns looking through the scope, first at the eagle and then at the nest. Although bald eagles winter in Nebraska and many others migrate through, nests were until recently quite rare; signs of courtship and breeding activity near a nest are still cause for excitement.

We're driving west again when I spot a large mass in the fork of a tree about a quarter mile off the road. It looks like a nest to me, and John agrees, "Yes, indeed." Fortunately, the next section line is a public road, so we pull in for a closer look and on the way spot an adult eagle perched in a second tree about fifty yards from the nest. We're scarcely out of the truck when John points east along the river to vast black wings flapping toward us. "I think we have a pair," he says. Yes, indeed. The second eagle lands on the edge of the nest, which looks like it is as wide as I am tall. We take turns at the spotting scope. The eagle turns its head, and its bright-yellow, massively hooked bill appears in full profile. It looks like it could tear through pavement. After a few minutes, the eagle pushes off from the nest and flies over to perch near the first bird. Not too near, though, as if they are still working out the terms of their relationship. We leave them to sort matters out in private. But I note the road sign as we leave, and so does John. We'll both be back.

The Johnson-2 plant, or J-2, is a humble-looking, sand-colored box that straddles a tree-lined ravine about thirty-five miles west of Kearney and two miles south of the Platte's natural channel. More striking perhaps than the building itself is the hill behind it and the flume — like a huge feeding tube — that descends the hill and enters the plant's west side. Through the flume, J-2 receives Platte River water that has traveled at least sixty miles through the canals and reservoirs of the Tri-County Irrigation Project to this spot, where it plummets 145 feet, creating enough force to spin a turbine beneath the electric generator.

J-2 and the whole network of Tri-County's canals, reservoirs, and power plants are operated by the Central Nebraska Public Power and Irrigation District, locally called "Central," because even the acronym CNPPID is unwieldy. Central really is, in many ways, central to life around here, not just because it provides irrigation water and generates electricity, but because it virtually has dominion over habitat on the Big Bend. Central's operations determine how much water flows through the central Platte and when. And in a river, water flows determine most everything else.

Inside the power plant, I look around as my companions pause at a folding table to sign the guest book. The building's interior feels like a cross between a factory and an old high school gymnasium. Of course it *is* a factory — for electricity — and the generator occupies most of the building. But what draw my attention are the vast windows on the east wall and a section of bleachers where visitors can sit and gaze. We walk over to see.

Just outside the window, low concrete walls line the tail-race, through which the river water, its work done, rushes out from beneath the building. About a half mile east, the water flows around a bend in the channel toward the point where it will return to the Platte, about three miles away. Above the concrete walls are steep banks of exposed soil, pock-marked with dozens of deep, golf ball–sized holes: a swallow colony. The bank swallows are wintering hundreds of miles away, but

I can picture how they must enliven this scene in the summer, swooping across the water in the narrow, green-shaded glade.

Today, however, the scene is different. The thick cottonwood trees that climb the banks are leafless and gray — but adorned with bald eagles. Eight of them . . . nine . . . we are all counting, each of us pointing out birds we think the others might have overlooked. Eagles congregate around the tailrace because here they are assured of not only open water but a steady supply of carp, all stunned by their trip past the turbine.

Carol has carried a picnic basket inside, and as we gather around her on the bleachers, she produces lunch. "Leftovers," she says dismissively, but what leftovers! Turkey and roast beef sandwiches on home-baked bread, apples, two types of chips, and a bag of dark-chocolate malted milk balls. And cloth napkins. The cold weather seems to have sharpened our appetites. With a napkin on one knee and binoculars on the other, I bite into roast beef and horseradish and sigh with pleasure, eating lunch with the eagles.

When the last malted milk ball is gone, I raise my binoculars again. The nearest eagle is just thirty yards away, and every detail is clear: the orange-yellow talons; body feathers that are actually dark, dark brown, not black; a piercing yellow eye. As I look, I feel a vague unease with my enjoyment of the scene. The pretty ravine, after all, is an artificial river, and these powerful, magnificent birds — symbols of wilderness to many North Americans — have been reduced to scavenging for the by-products of human engineering.

Or not. After all, the Platte River was probably good habitat for bald eagles even before the first dam or diversion. Sporadic trees along the riverbanks offered perches, and here and there, groundwater seeps created pockets of open water.

Furthermore, what shame is there in being opportunistic? In nature, the ends — survival — justify the means, and many species that have mastered exploitation of human habitat are not only surviving but thriving: robins, raccoons, white-tailed deer . . . and sandhill cranes. Why not eagles, too?

John has set up his spotting scope, zeroed in on one of the eagles, and is inviting a mother and her two children to take a look. "The focus is on the top," I hear him say. What I've learned from watching John is that when you share what you see with other people, you begin to notice more yourself.

I wander over to the guest-book table, where a retired Central employee tells me that he and a colleague have volunteered for years to serve as hosts here on winter weekends so that visitors can see the eagles. He moves his battered thermos out of the way and flips through the guest book's pages, showing me that although it's quiet this morning, they often see fifty visitors in a single day. Also on the table are three stacks of information brochures about Central. Two are guides to boating and fishing on Lake McConaughy and the district's smaller reservoirs. The third describes Central's history and operations. One page summarizes Central's role in managing fish and wildlife habitat on its properties and managing water releases for the benefit of wildlife downstream. Another page lists recreational opportunities available on the district's 36,000-plus acres of impounded waters: "boating, fishing, water-skiing, sailing, jet-skiing, swimming . . ." All of this on the borrowed waters of a prairie river.

On the drive back to Kearney, we take the interstate; although our distance and speed make it unlikely that we'll see eagles, I'm still scanning the treetops. While I scan, I think about Rick Bass's admonition in *The Lost Grizzlies*, a book that is as much about vanishing wilderness as it is about the quest for bears. "Don't coast," Bass tells himself as he contemplates the human forces that threaten the world's last wild places. "Don't blink, don't look away, don't be slothful. Keep your eyes open. Look closely everywhere. Pay attention!"

We have no wilderness here, only wild birds that might be part of some distant wilderness when they fly north in the spring. Perhaps that is part of what we celebrate when we count eagles or watch cranes and arctic geese: a connection to a wilderness we might never see. The birds are proof that the wilderness exists somewhere and a promise that when they fly north, our imaginations can fly with them.

January 11 is Aldo Leopold's birthday. It is time for a walk beside the river. As I cross the parking lot at Rowe Sanctuary, I wonder, as I often do in January, whether there is anything to see.

I don't require much. In the opening lines of *A Sand County Almanac*, Leopold extols the uneventful winter walk as one with few distractions: "January observation can be almost as simple and peaceful as snow, and almost as continuous as cold. There is time not only to see who has done what, but to speculate why."

The bobwhites are huddled and squeaking softly in the woodlot behind the sanctuary's old farmhouse. As I pass, I hear them stir, and the squeaks begin to sound like squeals. I brace myself for the explosive flurry of a panicked covey, but instead they scurry away through the undergrowth.

The sky is clear blue but for a few silvery wisps of cloud. The stems of last summer's prairie plants poke through a thin crust of snow. A light breeze from the north ruffles the Canada wild rye, whose droopy, fluffy-looking seed heads bob gently. The big blue and Indian grass stems, bare of seed and offering less resistance to the wind, tremble rather than sway, glowing gold and russet in the sunshine.

At the river's edge, I settle on a hewn-log bench and, in the mass of wood, feel the day's chill for the first time. Two or three dozen mallards are muttering in the warm-water slough by the far riverbank, nearly hidden from my view by a series of sandbars. While most mallards winter in the southern United States or Mexico, many stay along the Platte all winter, so long as they can find open water. From time to time, a few ducks take flight, circle briefly, and return, while a voice or two rises from the slough in what hunters term a "come-back call": *Qua-a-a-a, qua-qua-qua*. Mallards are paired at this time of year, and whenever a hen flies, she is accompanied at least by her mate and sometimes by an additional, bachelor drake seeking a chance to pass on his genes. The ends, I suppose, justify the means.

Though the ducks have found open water, at least half of the river flows under lumpy, snowy ice that is slowly succumbing to the current. I hear crunching and rattling as water flows under and around the thinning ice ledge. Floating twigs, tubers, and other debris grind along the rotting edges, and broken-off ice chunks hang up and form temporary dams where water piles up and then streams across its own frozen surface.

I turn my head toward a slight fluttering sound, hardly more than a whisper. A few feet away, at my eye level, a brown-streaked song sparrow perches on a grass stalk and cocks its head, looking me over. I am either unthreatening or uninteresting; the sparrow hops sideways down the stalk and melts into the tall brown grass.

Across the river two crows *caw-caw* to each other and in tandem churn west along the treetops, changing places repeatedly. I try to puzzle out what seems like a game of tag, but it's hard to guess a motive when I can't tell which of the identical black birds is "it."

They vanish beyond the tree line, and I ramble downstream to see what else is new. Not much is new in January, but I do find something old in the willow-and-dogwood grove, something I overlooked when the shrubs were covered with leaves: dozens of birds' nests. The thick stand of seven- and eight-foot shrubs must seem ideal to nesting song birds. It's about fifty yards from fresh water and surrounded by grasses that, in the summer, offer a buffet of seeds and insects. And it's sheltered all summer by thick foliage, so that someone like me could walk past on the path ten times or more and never suspect the concentration and variety of intricately engineered nests hidden a few feet away. Now, standing among the naked branches, I can see twelve nests from one spot, just by turning my head. Their resilience is astonishing, for nearly all are intact after months of autumn and winter wind gusts that buckled road signs and upended sheds. The few nests that do show damage appear to be more than a year old. I wander from nest to nest, feeling how firmly each is attached to the branches, touching the soft insides. Two nests are easily identifiable as goldfinch construction: tidy cups softly lined with thistle down that are so tightly woven they feel like papier-mâché. Another, made from tangles of long golden grasses, is strung up like a sagging hammock; that's an orchard oriole. A deep cup of tangled grasses, twigs, and strips of bark might belong to a gray catbird; I've seen them around here. Others are a mystery. Although all these nests are in the same grove, surrounded by the same plants and building materials, each species shows a preference for particular combinations of grasses, twigs, and leaves. I page through my field guide, comparing photos of nests made by dickcissels, yellow warblers, and several species of sparrows, asking not "why" but "who." The answer might come in the spring. Songbirds do not generally reuse nests, but it's a safe bet that they, or other members of their species, will return to this grove. Now that I know they are here, I'll pay attention.

I look up at the sky. It seems like the sort of day for a red-tailed hawk or two to trace circles in the air. But no. Although I have not seen much, I am content to go home and back to my desk. Sometimes even a short walk is enough to reset the mind's gyre.

A week later, I am back at the hewn-log bench, where I wait to meet fellow volunteer and writer Alan Bartels. The temperature has stayed below freezing, and the river is almost entirely covered by ice, although fault lines are forming, thanks to the bright sunshine. The ice groans and makes knocking sounds, as if someone were locked in and trying to get out.

I turn and walk toward Alan, who is approaching me on the path. Head and shoulders taller than me, Alan has dark eyes and an air of reserve that verges on melancholy. "Hey," he says, and we walk in silence for a minute but are soon comparing notes about what we saw on the way here: a shrike on a power line, eagles in the cornfield across the road.

We set out for the west trail — he with a camera, and I with binoculars. The trees between the path and the river block our view of the water for a while, and the only sound is the snow crunching beneath our feet. Tracks — all sorts of inhuman feet — intertwine before us. We bend down to examine prints that look like tiny hands — probably raccoon, we agree, although the shapes are blurred by melting and refreezing, so there's some room for doubt. Winter walks often amount to this; we spend less time observing what is happening around us — because little is happening — and more time examining clues and trying to surmise what must have happened before.

Alan is an observant person who has followed his interests all over Nebraska, especially to the Sandhills — or any place where turtles live. But he always makes time to come back here during the crane migration and lead a few groups to the observation blinds. He was here to lead volunteer training sessions during my first spring at Rowe, and we called him the Turtle Guy. I wondered, "How many turtles can there be in a place like Nebraska?" The answer was "plenty." I just had to keep my eyes open.

As we pass an opening in the trees, two mallards fly above the river. "Look, something *is* alive," Alan says with a brief laugh. Sometimes in January it's easier than usual to forget how much life is still around us. Reptiles and amphibians are hibernating. Birds that feed on insects are spending the winter where they can find food. Mammals are hard to spot at any time of year. But the tracks and trails in the snow tell stories of ongoing life. A small hole in the snow marks the entrance of a mouse's tiny tunnel. Rabbit tracks appear here and there — large hind-foot tracks in front of the tiny forefeet. And right before us on the path, the scene of a small calamity. The snow is trampled and strewn about, scattered with clumps of feathers and splashes of blood. The work of a hawk, we guess by the size of the imprints. But who died? We study the remnants; Alan takes a picture. From the brush beside the path comes a chorus of worried-sounding squeaks. Ah. We look at each other, eyebrows raised. One dead quail.

We take a side path through the trees to the water's edge and look around. The ice, strangely, is at two heights. The frozen shelf along the bank, where we attempt to stand and inch forward, seems to cover semifrozen sand and wetland. The ice sheet that covers the rest of the channel is half a hand span higher, forming a gap through which we can see the rushing water several inches below. The water bounces along in a way that explains the knocking I heard earlier downstream. Any turbulence — and there's plenty in the channel by the log bench — would have created an effect like a tall man banging his head against the roof of a shed.

Alan is squatting by the ice gap, taking photos. "Looks like the water level dropped a lot," he observes.

Slightly chagrined, I answer, "Uh huh," as if I had noticed that, too.

When he lowers his camera and looks out across the river, I imagine we are seeing the same thing — ten thousand warbling, milling cranes standing in this water and even right where we stand. For we are near a favorite roost, and the birds often crowd up onto this flat bank. I know that Alan looks forward to the cranes' return, as I do, to experience once again that display of the earth's bounty. "Seeing them makes me feel we haven't destroyed everything," he says. "They give me hope."

Alan knows this sanctuary as well as anybody, and still he studies his surroundings as if heeding Rick Bass's instruction: "Look closely everywhere." He pauses to inspect the beaver lodge he has seen countless times; he follows deer tracks with his eyes to see where they lead; when we pass a stack of PVC drainpipes — a stack I overlooked completely on earlier walks here — he squats and peers in to check for skunks and then lifts a few pipes to see if other creatures might scurry out.

I think about Aldo Leopold's peaceful January walks — walks with time to "speculate why." Why speculate? Because we are storytelling, story-seeking creatures. Through story, we interpret our own lives and the lives around us.

On the way back to the parking lot, I am looking up at the cottonwood branches overhanging the path. I have been keeping an eye on two oriole nests to see how long they last. The older one has survived three winters and two major ice storms and is still intact. When it finally falls, I want to be around to pick it up. Just before we reach the path to the observation blind, we spot a nest I have never noticed before; it's cup shaped like a robin's and attached to a horizontal branch right above the path. I might have missed it but for the naked corncob propped inside like a swizzle stick. Alan takes a picture. I smile and imagine him, ever the naturalist, showing the photograph to friends and challenging them to speculate — why?

11 *Wonders Close to Home*

This is the month when winter starts to fade. February in Nebraska is a time of contemplation, like the hour before sunrise, when darkness dissolves and the world begins to stir. Today the snow and ice are dissolving in bright sunshine that's as startling and exhilarating as daylight that floods a dark bedroom when the curtains are thrown open.

Near the river a clump of rusty brown moves on the snow beneath a big maple tree. The fox squirrel digs urgently, his back arched and head down. He roots around for a few seconds, pops up on his haunches to look around, and then digs some more. Then he bounds to a new spot and digs again. Some children's stories suggest that squirrels dig like this because they've forgotten where they buried last fall's nuts. Maybe so. But one wonders how squirrels could remain so numerous if they were so utterly incompetent at providing for themselves. In any case, it's forty-five degrees and sunny, so most of the snow will not last the day. The squirrel could take a break. But that's not what squirrels do.

The Platte River's south channel is mostly frozen; a thick trickle marks the main current's winding course between sandbars and under the trestle bridge. Small puddles dot the layer of ice. A sensible person — certainly a child, who feels no guilt about whiling away a few hours — would stand here on the bridge until afternoon to watch the puddles widen and see the current slowly eat away at the ice ledge. The gap within the ice will soon widen enough to hold a few ducks . . . and then a few more.

Nearby, a small flurry stirs the naked trees and shrubs beside the path. I turn and see that it's a bright-blue flurry: two dozen bluebirds hop back and forth between branches and from tree to tree. Most of Nebraska's eastern bluebirds migrate south for the winter, but a small number stay around in the cold months, including these hardy individuals, who probably emerged from their shared roost in a hollow tree to enjoy the warm day and pick at some berries exposed by the melting snow. The females are much paler blue than the males, but they all look like blossoms against the winter's gray and white.

Into their midst flies a downy woodpecker, whose undulating flight reminds me of a jump rope swinging back and forth in "Shallows," an old neighborhood sidewalk game from my childhood. The black-and-white downy adds little to the trailside palette, except for the patch of scarlet feathers at the back of his head. It bobs as he works his way along a peeling twig, worrying the bark and muttering, "*pip, pip.*"

A half mile away, I find the north channel open, flooded with meltwater from the canyon of snow that lines its banks. The sparkling canyon wall is undercut where the channel bends, and sometime today it will collapse, like a tiny glacier calving in a bay. Leaning over the bridge, I guess that if I were to wade in, the frigid water would reach my armpits. It's remarkably clear, though; marble-sized pebbles — orange, slate colored, and brown — show clearly beneath four feet of water.

I am still looking down when the noise begins overhead. A squeaking chorus of "*Yike! Yike! Yike!*" announces a flock of two hundred snow geese flying west along the river, and then another flock, and then a third. Their white bodies and black wing tips flash in the sunlight, and I feel a thrill of anticipation.

Walking back on the trail, I hear another uproar overhead and crouch low before looking up. These birds are dark: Canada geese and their cousins, cackling geese. They fly so low I need no binoculars to make out their white "chin straps" and black tail feathers. Their two-pitch call, "*Ha-ronk, ha-ronk,*" sounds joyful to my human ears. But it's not the only sound; as the birds pass low over my head, I hear the soft rush of air through their flight feathers.

Sight may be the sense on which we most heavily rely, but for some reason, simply looking is not enough. Toddlers, despite their parents' refrain of, "Look, don't touch," demonstrate our innate craving for sensory experience. Years after our elders have extracted the last pebble or ballpoint pen from our curious mouths, most of us still want to experience the world's wonders through more than one sense. Who could buy a loaf of fresh bread and resist the impulse to open the bag for a whiff? Velvet curtains and angora sweaters just ask to be touched. And at the ocean there's no question that we must toss off our shoes and wade into the surf. It's not so easy to touch a flock of wild birds. But sitting alone on the trail and hearing their flight, whispered just to me, I feel as though I've come close.

"*Ha-ronk, ha-ronk,*" they call again, and my mind responds, "Hurry up, spring. Hurry up!"

Back at the car, I am unlocking the door when something moves at the edge of my sight and tumbles down the windshield. I reach for a small, dark piece of fluff: a goose feather. It's so airy it feels like almost nothing against my cheek. It flutters without a breeze, with just my breath. I lay it on the passenger seat — something to occupy me at the red lights in town — and pull out of the parking lot.

In the field by the highway, a farmer swings a sledge to break the weakening ice in a water tank. This afternoon or tomorrow, a truck will probably lumber into the field and unload a herd of cattle to graze the cornstalks. And in a few more days, the cattle will have sandhill cranes for company. At this thought, I smile and start to wave to the farmer — a "spring-is-coming" sort of wave. But he is intent on his work. Winter in Nebraska does not so easily release its grip.

When I arrive for an evening visit at Rowe Sanctuary, the presages are in the sky: a V-shaped flock of a hundred honking, squeaking geese flies west along the river. Then another flock passes. The music changes to an echoing trumpet, and here is a wavy line of cranes, following the path of the geese. It seems a shame to go indoors, but on the other hand, we can't spend all of the next two months outdoors, just listening to birds.

I am here to visit with Steve and Cyndi King and to hear about what Steve calls "the Huckleberry Days." Before stepping inside, I look around at the grounds and at the river. If not for the house and shed, it would be easy to forget that this land was once a real farm, occupied by real people.

Steve is one of the real people who grew up in the little white farmhouse. Now he and Cyndi, like me, are part of the group who make ourselves at home in the Iain Nicolson Center and gather regularly around the table in the staff kitchen to share potluck meals and stories. Steve and Cyndi, now in late middle age, have been together since their college years in Kearney. They still have the fair-haired good looks of a midwestern homecoming king and queen and the kind of body language that makes you believe in lasting love. As we settle at the table in the kitchen and Steve uncorks a bottle of wine, I picture sitting down to dinner each night for eight weeks with the calls of thousands of cranes echoing outside the back door. After weeks and weeks, or years and years, maybe the masses of birds would seem as ordinary as the wind, as unsurprising as a river of sand.

Steve tells me his father and grandfather farmed this land together. Cattle grazed the field to the east. The field across the road, now in corn, was planted in milo; west of that, it was hay meadow all the way to the south channel, where, in those days, water still flowed and grazing cattle kept the banks free from trees.

For the children on farms up and down this stretch of the river in the 1950s, the Platte was a communal playground. Youngsters roamed and explored with a freedom that today's suburban parents might find shocking. "We were just all river kids," Steve recalls, "and I don't think our folks worried very much about us."

When the water was high, the men sat on the bank with fishing rods while the youngsters learned to "read the current" and recognize where the deep spots were likely to be. Steve and the other kids floated among the sloughs that were downstream on the Tripletts' place. Now that area is part of the sanctuary, a part where I frequently walk between the sand ridges and have never gotten my boots wet.

During the growing season, when water was diverted to

irrigation canals, Steve recalls that the river dried up completely. I ask about the weeds that nowadays crowd the channel when it's dry, and he shakes his head. "It was pure sand," he says, and then he looks rather wistful and says they played baseball in the dry channel. "You could hit a grounder, and it'd just roll forever."

Early autumn brought the end of irrigation season and the end of empty channels on the Platte. The gates closed on irrigation canals, the water rolled downstream, and people on the river *knew*. They smelled the water's approach, Steve tells me. I think my eyebrows rise, and he just smiles. But how else would they sense it before it even arrived? Someone would shout, "Water's coming!" and the youngsters would dash outside to meet it.

The water flowed into the fall, into duck-hunting season. The farmhouse — now a gathering place for volunteer naturalists and, for several years, the sanctuary headquarters where birdwatchers gathered — was a hub during Steve's childhood, too. He recalls his mother rising at four o'clock in the morning to cook breakfast for friends and neighbors before they pulled on their hip boots and waded out to the several hunting blinds in the middle of the river.

And what about those other birds, I ask, the big gray ones that come in the spring? "They were annoying to us," he says, straight-faced. I pause, perplexed. "They were noisy when they came," he says and grins mischievously at my apparent confusion. "And the silence was annoying when they left." I imagine lying in bed, listening to the cranes warbling and bugling all night long and roaring into the sky each morning. To me it sounds wildly exotic, but for a river kid snuggled in his bed, the cranes' voices were just part of how the world was supposed to be. "You sure missed them when they were gone," he says.

But in cities just a few miles away, plenty of people never

noticed, including Cyndi, who grew up in Grand Island. "I didn't even know cranes existed until we got married," she says. Her first encounter with the strange-looking birds was during a springtime visit to her new mother-in-law. They looked like huge, gray flamingoes, Cyndi thought; she urged Mrs. King to hurry and look out the window before they flew away. The older woman just shrugged nonchalantly and said, "They'll be here for a month."

It was a surprising blow when Steve's father and grandfather sold the farm in 1975. Although he had prepared for a teaching career, Steve always envisioned returning to the farm someday. The businessmen who bought the place perhaps knew more about their business than about farming. Steve says they plowed up the pasture by the river, breaking sod in the wet meadow to the southwest and planting everything to corn. "They planted right up to the buildings," he says, shaking his head. The barn was in the way, so they tore it down and burned the lumber. I wince to think of corn rows in fields where milkweed, big bluestem, and Indian grass now belong. And I'm not the one who grew up here.

The National Audubon Society bought the property in 1988, expanding the size of Rowe Sanctuary. And that might have been the end of the Kings' connection with the place, if Cyndi had not dropped by the farmhouse one day about seven or eight years later just to see how things looked. Inside the house, which had become the sanctuary office, she met the director, Paul Tebbel. She liked Paul, liked his ideas for bringing people here to see the cranes, and she liked being at the sanctuary. So she came back. Brought Steve's sisters to visit. Came back again. And eventually began to volunteer when help was needed. Then she brought Steve.

These days, Steve leads crane watchers to the observation

blinds in the spring, and Cyndi is a regular in the lobby, welcoming visitors and helping in the gift shop. And when I lead a tour on the same mornings as Steve, I sometimes point him out to members of my group. "See the man over there in the brown jacket? He grew up on the farm that was right here." Eyes grow wide. "Can you imagine?" someone almost always asks. I like to try.

Driving away from the sanctuary, toward the great orange moon that hangs just above the horizon, I try again to imagine how it must have been. To get off the school bus and walk into the house past a yard full of grazing, dancing birds. To chafe at the silent dawn after the last bird has flown north. To sit for hours in a cottonwood tree on the bank, studying the current.

What must it be like to know a place so intimately that you can *smell* the water coming? No matter how much I read, ask, and watch, Steve understands things about this river that I never will. Still, for a few minutes tonight, I became one of those river kids, lying in the streamside grass and watching the clouds or playing ball in the sandy channel. And for all the times I have seen this stretch of river, after tonight it will never look quite the same. Even with the car window closed, I can hear voices across the river. Children are laughing and shouting as one of them races across the sand, chasing a ground ball that rolls and rolls.

Just before February ends, I take a morning walk at the river. It's colder now than when the month began, and the wind is barreling out of the north at thirty miles an hour or so, except when it gusts more strongly. If I were a colorful banner, I'd be flapping cheerily, making crisp snapping sounds in the wind. But I am a woman with long hair and an occasionally short temper, and the snapping sound is me, grousing at the gale that shoots chills up my spine and tosses my hair into my eyes, making them tear. The temperature is near freezing, and so am I. For a minute I consider giving up and going home. But I'm here, so I might as well walk, even if there is nothing to see on such a day.

And yet there is always something to see. In the meadow on my right, a harrier glides just above the tops of the tall grass. It pauses in the air, hovering, while some tiny rodent is no doubt cowering under the thatch. And if the cowering rodent has a sense of time, it might wonder, as I do, that the tumultuous air can hold a one-pound bird aloft in one spot for so many impossibly long seconds. Finally, the raptor spreads its long wings and soars away. The rodent and I exhale and move on.

In the cornfield on my left is a line about a hundred yards away, where the color seems to change. Through my binoculars I see a throng of geese waddling among the rows: Canadas and white and slate-colored snow geese. They cover at least three acres. The Platte River valley is beginning to fill again with a torrent of birds.

Ducks, in twos and threes, crisscross the sky above the river. On the water, I think I see ring-necked ducks. But they're behind the trees, and the wind blurs my sight again with tears, so even with binoculars, I can't say for sure. So I walk until I find a game trail — a narrow path worn by deer — through the undergrowth and into a ditch perpendicular to the river. On my knees at the bottom of the ditch, I'm unable to see the channel — which means the *ducks* can't see *me*. I begin to crawl, glad at last for the wind, which drowns out the crackle of dry grass.

Small flocks of Canada geese fly overhead almost constantly. They honk, and I crouch lower. But they are apparently not talking about me, because the ducks stay in the water and the geese stay on course for the sloughs a half mile upstream. Broken twigs litter the ditch and stab my hands and knees. But I am committed now, and it can't be much farther. Finally, where the ditch meets the bank, I cautiously raise my head and shoulders and see . . . nothing. Flat on the ground again, I inch up, up, out of the ditch to a thick wooden post at the corner of a fenced pasture and can go no farther. I peek up and am almost unnerved to see hundreds of ducks just yards away. I can't exactly hide behind an eight-inch fence post. But it's about the same shade as my brown coat, so I lean against it and make like a very wide post. The ducks stay calm, so they must be falling for it. Some two hundred mallards and northern pintails float on the water. The mallard drakes' dark-green heads gleam in the sunlight, and the graceful pintails are regal, with their tall, curved necks and spiked tail feathers. But it's the ring-necked ducks that I have come to see. I like pintails and mallards, and I like the tiny green-winged teal that dabble near the shore. But I am infatuated with ring-necked ducks. To me, the drakes are the handsomest of waterfowl, with black heads and backs; their sides are pearl gray and white. But most striking are their gray bills, outlined in white and tipped with black, as if adorned with ceremonial paint. And the ceremony today is courtship.

With two males for every female, the drakes are competing to show off their fine looks. They splash their bills repeatedly in the river. Droplets fly about. One drake rears up in the water to spread and flap his wings. They flash — black above, pale below. Then another bird rises and flaps, while others continue to splash.

Usually, migrating birds are more skittish than those who are settled in familiar surroundings. If I saw these ducks on their wintering grounds, I might stay longer, without worrying that I would frighten them into energy-wasting flight. But migration stopovers are unfamiliar territory. The wind may be masking my presence, but it also knocks me against the fence post so that I can't keep still. Rather than risk spooking the birds, I slip back down to the bottom of the ditch and begin to crawl away. Now unable to see if I am visible to the birds in the channel behind me, I try to crawl lower than before. The wind pelts my face and pours under my collar and down my back. The cold knifes across my shoulders, and my hips and knees ache. But I scoot forward. Suddenly, mirth overcomes misery, and I collapse on the ground, laughing silently. When I first came to Nebraska, I despaired of finding magic in a landscape so foreign from the one I had called home. But at this moment, there is no place I would rather be than here, lying face down in the dirt, plotting my course between brambles and poison ivy, beside a river that's alive with wild ducks.

At nightfall when I return to the trestle bridge, the wind has calmed to just a breeze but still blows from the north, so it carries the whine of the interstate traffic across the river valley. It also carries the sound I have come to hear: geese.

In truth, I came to *see* the geese, to watch them fly to the river at dusk, but I am late. The stars are winking in the black sky, and the geese are already on their roosts. The yelping, honking tumult rises and falls in waves around me on the path and on the south channel. The water is high tonight; moonlight sparkles on the dimples and eddies that form in the intertwining currents. Water rushes against the bridge's wooden pilings and briefly competes with the clamor of the birds. But their voices rise again to a shrill roar, and I squint into the shadows, perplexed that the source of such an uproar — easily a thousand birds — can be invisible.

I should be content just to listen. I rest my elbows on the

bridge railing and prop my chin in my hands. Every few minutes, headlights on the Highway 10 bridge flicker in the distance. The river throws back the moon's borrowed sunlight. Nothing else moves. And it occurs to me that of all the seven billion people in the world, I might be the only person standing still to hear these thousand geese sing vespers on the Platte River. Five miles away in Kearney and just a mile downstream on Kilgore Road, people are washing their supper dishes or watching television and have relinquished this blessing to me alone.

My first impulse is to deride their indifference — indifference to geese, to cranes, to the world around them. But I too have been guilty of indifference. The sun that gives our planet life offers up an utterly unique show of colors and shadows every morning and night, but more often than not, I am too busy to see. I never looked for the nest of the Carolina wren that sang all last summer in my yard. And I've plucked a hundred or more sprouting samaras from my garden without once thinking to shout praise for a small green seed that can spin sunlight and water into wood and perfect maple leaves.

When we were children, the world was a vast, astonishing place that we expected to explore and keep exploring until we had learned everything there was to know. My friends and I were in training to mush across the Canadian tundra, hike the western badlands, and paddle through alligator swamps in the South. In the meantime, our backyards were our wilderness. We were wild horses galloping on the plains, little animals hiding from eagles overhead, and heroic Amazons scaling mountainsides.

But we grew up and settled down. We got responsible jobs, earning money for clothes and cars, so that we could dress up and drive to jobs that would pay for our clothes and our cars. There was no longer much time for wonder.

By the time I was ready to explore the world, I realized there was no place where someone else had not already been. There is no place left on earth that has not felt the careless hand of the human race. And almost no place has escaped being tamed or tainted. Even Antarctica has become a "destination."

If human footprints are everywhere, are we through discovering the world's marvels? Only if we stop looking. The answer, I think, is to travel not farther but deeper. To the discoverer, I would recommend, "Start with the ground beneath your feet."

A crescendo of honks and squeaks follows me as I begin the walk back to my car. But the geese are neither calling me back nor saying good-bye. I don't exist in their world, and that's as it should be.

The city of Kearney glows on the nighttime horizon, and the rising glare as I approach Second Avenue makes me feel I've traveled a long way in just twelve miles. I drive up the tunnel of lights, through offerings of new cars, dinner, or a night's lodging — the same cars, dinners, and lodgings I could buy everywhere else in the United States.

I park in the driveway of my darkened house, and I reach into the glove box for my purse. Under it, my fingers find something else — something so soft it feels like nothing. This fluffy bit of goose feather may have spent the winter in Mexico or on the Louisiana coast. But here it will stay, while its owner continues to Hudson Bay, perhaps, or to the Yukon. I carry it into the house and set it on the bookshelf between the broken antler and the fritillary's wing. I don't mean to keep it very long, but I'll probably pick it up from time to time and examine its dreamlike softness, until one day when a breeze catches it and it vanishes like some childish fancy.

12 *Swept Up, Still and Again*

MARCH

The sunlight in the western sky strikes my rearview mirror through the cloud of dust my car kicks up as I tear down Kilgore Road. I glance at my watch — six thirty. To reach the north blind, I have a ten-minute walk across a wet meadow that the cranes use as an evening roost before they fly to the river for the night. I must cross the meadow and be in the blind well before birds start to land there, or I risk frightening them all away.

Given the rare chance to spend an evening alone in the north blind, I should have taken more care to leave home on time. But during the migration, it seems there's never enough time to see and do everything, so I am constantly running late, juggling and rushing from one thing to another, trying to . . . to . . . Stop. Take a breath. Enjoy. A group of cranes flies past leisurely.

The gated parking place comes into view as I reach the wet meadow, and I'm both relieved and disappointed. I see no cranes yet, so it's safe to walk. But what I do see is a car parked in my spot. There goes my evening alone.

While opening the gate, I look toward the blind and see

movement through one of the windows — someone in an orange jacket. Small groups of cranes, three birds, six birds, fly overhead, landing not in the meadow but across the road in a pasture. I park in the mowed grass beside the Subaru with Minnesota plates and guess that it belongs to Ed and Sil Pembleton. If I can't be alone, at least I will be in good company. Ed worked for the Audubon Society in the 1980s and '90s and was one of the river's guardians. They're part of this place.

I walk across the meadow, feeling slightly guilty; they, too, were probably expecting some solitude. Within a few minutes, though, the music of the meadow crowds out any worries. Cranes' voices ring through the air, twirling with meadow-larks' songs. The grass beneath my feet is lumpy and unevenly cropped. In some years, this meadow is mowed for hay, but last summer cattle grazed here. The ground, too, is uneven, rippled with abandoned river channels that I cross at an angle on the short-mowed walking path toward the blind.

The north blind is a two-story wooden box with an enclosed staircase, like a steep tunnel, to the upper story. The door swings open as I climb the steps. I know Ed and Sil just slightly, but they greet me warmly, as if we were old friends. "We didn't recognize you at first," Ed says, "but we watched how you opened the gate, and knew you belonged here."

I glance around the blind; Ed and Sil have already opened the plywood window flaps on all four sides, so we can see in every direction. Feeling a bit shy, as if I had intruded on their privacy, I shrug my backpack onto a shelf in the northeast corner, on the far side of the blind from Sil's pack and Ed's tripod.

We whisper now and then, pointing out a kingfisher, a pair of green-winged teal, the northern harrier perched conspicuously on a nearby fence post. But mostly we're quiet, and so is the river, its water riffling gently. Two mallards paddle silently in the slough beneath the south windows. From time to time, cranes fly past in small, wispy flocks. Most of the activity, though, is still in the north — away from the river and across the road from our parked cars, where cranes continue to land in the pasture.

By seven o'clock the view through the north window starts to change. Wisps thicken into solid, bold lines of birds. Lines skim westward; others skim east. The lines cross, blend, and drift down, beginning to settle onto the meadow.

The sun sinks lower, clouds thicken to swirls tinged with lavender and pink, and the flocks of cranes above the meadow thicken, too. East of us, a flock twists and folds in on itself like a whirlpool as it drifts toward the ground. Thousands of birds flood the sky to our north and pour into the meadow, like water tumbling over a dam. The field churns with gray flapping wings and milling bodies.

A few cranes begin to land on the river. Against the pink sunset, they look like black arcs, tipping right and then left as they angle into the wind. Wings out, heads up, feet down. Just before reaching the water, they raise their heads upright and brake with two or three flaps of their fanned wings.

A sudden roar rises from the north. We turn to peek out the north window as the whole field becomes a rising, boiling cloud that surges toward the river. Cranes' shouts roll toward us in waves.

From a field upstream, tens of thousands of birds take flight, even as more flocks pour down into the meadows around us. The energy within the blind, previously loose and easy as we aimlessly watched the river, has shifted, becoming tight and focused. Everything but cranes has vanished. Above the river, some flocks are so thick they seem to be, not individual birds, but a single organism, a single consciousness. Other flocks pass in tangled skeins or a few thin strands. Time moves at some pace that cannot be measured by a clock. Soon, or perhaps much later, the sun sinks from view.

In the dark, a hand touches my shoulder. I turn, and Sil points silently to the west window, where, near Fort Kearny, flocks swirl thickly against the horizon's last dim glow. Ed, too, seems transfixed. I shake my head, marveling mostly at the cranes but also at us. Among the three of us, the morning and evening hours we've spent on the Platte must number in the thousands, and still the sense of wonder feels fresh.

The bugling continues as the sky becomes fully dark, and still through binoculars we watch black flocks fly past and swirl down onto the water. Then in the space of a minute, the movement slows and ceases. The calls shift from high-pitched excitement to the steady flow of contact calls that the cranes make all night. The change feels as abrupt as the drop of a theater curtain.

There's no need to speak. Ed lifts the plywood flap to close the window before him and turns the toggle. I reach to close my window, and the blind grows darker as we make our way around, silently closing windows one by one until we stand in blackness. There's a soft rustle of fabric and then a second rustle, as Sil and I pull on our backpacks. "Ready?" Ed whispers. "Ready," we both whisper in reply.

We tiptoe down the staircase tunnel and emerge beneath a spangled cupola of stars — millions of stars clotted here and there in shining knots. After the streaming, swirling movement of cranes, the stillness of the sky is nearly dizzying. It is impossible not to look up at heavens that seem more white than black.

Ed leads the way back; Sil and I linger, pausing every few

steps to listen and look around. From time to time, rustling shadows fly overhead; a few honks and bugles ring out. A single white-fronted goose calls in the darkness. Several times, I almost whisper to Sil, "It's so hard to leave," but I don't want to make a sound. Still, something inside me aches, like a good-bye, as if I will never see a night like this again.

Near the cars, we catch up with Ed, who points up. "There's Orion."

"We don't have stars like this in St. Paul," Sil says softly.

"No," I say. "We're keeping them all here in Nebraska."

I get the gate, feeling for the latch. Ed will close it on the way out; he, too, could operate it with his eyes closed.

Despite the cold, I open the window as I drive slowly along the dirt road. If I see headlights, I'll turn on my own; if not, I know this lonely dirt road well enough to navigate by feel and by the stars. The taillights in my rearview mirror fade, and I stop the car to get out for one last look. Leaning against the door, I lift my face toward the laughing calls of yet another flock of northbound white-fronted geese, probably the last ones I'll hear this spring. Their departure feels like a calendar page flipping over. When the next page flips, the cranes will be kettling up. Another page, and the last cranes will have flown from our sight. But tonight in the north blind, the calendar stopped — briefly and forever — as we stood beneath and within the living whirlwind of a hundred thousand beating wings, and tonight we'll all sleep beneath the same sky.

Allen, Robert Porter. *The Whooping Crane*. National Audubon Society
   Research Report 3. New York: National Audubon Society, 1952.
"Audubon Is Establishing Platte Wildlife Sanctuary." *Kearney Hub*,
   April 2, 1973, 1.
Bass, Rick. *The Lost Grizzlies*. New York: Houghton Mifflin, 1995.
Bellrose, Frank. *Ducks, Geese, and Swans of North America*. Harrisburg
   PA: Stackpole, 1976.
Campbell, Joseph, and Bill Moyers. *The Power of Myth 2: The Message
   of the Myth*. Audiocassette. Prince Frederick MD: HighBridge, 1992.
Cather, Willa. *Lucy Gayheart*. New York: Knopf, 1961.
———. *O Pioneers!* New York: Bantam Classic, 1989.
Central Nebraska Public Power and Irrigation District. *Central Nebraska
   Public Power and Irrigation District: Irrigation, Hydropower, Recre-
   ation, Wildlife Habitat*. Holdrege NE: CNPPID, n.d.
———. "CNPPID Irrigated Area." http://www.cnppid.com/wp-content
   /uploads/2014/01/Irrigated_area.pdf.
———. "Project Maps: The Central Nebraska Public Power and Irrigation
   District, Project Maps." http://www.cnppid.com/operations/project
   -maps-2/.
Chronic, Halka. *Roadside Geology of Colorado*. Missoula: Mountain
   Press Publishing, 1980.
Conant, Roger, and Joseph T. Collins. *A Field Guide to Reptiles and
   Amphibians: Eastern/Central North America*. 3rd ed. Boston: Hough-
   ton, 1998.
Condon, Steven M. *Geologic Studies of the Platte River, South-Central
   Nebraska and Adjacent Areas — Geologic Maps, Subsurface Study,*

and Geologic History. Reston VA: United States Geological Survey, 2005.

Converse, Caroline Langman. *I Remember Papa*. Sunland CA: Cecil L. Anderson, 1949.

Currier, Paul J., Gary R. Lingle, and John G. VanDerwalker. *Migratory Bird Habitat on the Platte and North Platte Rivers in Nebraska*. Grand Island: Platte River Whooping Crane Critical Habitat Maintenance Trust, 1985.

Denver Water. "Collection System." http://www.denverwater.org/Supply Planning/WaterSupply/CollectionSystem.

Echeverria, John D. "No Success Like Failure: The Platte River Collaborative Watershed Planning Process." *William and Mary Environmental Law and Policy Review* 25 (2001): 559–604.

Evans, Howard Ensign. *The Natural History of the Long Expedition to the Rocky Mountains (1819–1820)*. New York: Oxford University Press, 1997.

Frith, Charles R. "The Ecology of the Platte River as Related to Sandhill Cranes and Other Waterfowl in South-Central Nebraska." Master's thesis, Kearney State College, Kearney, Nebraska, 1974.

Gil-Weir, Karine, and Paul Johnsgard. "The Whooping Cranes: Survivors Against All Odds." *Prairie Fire Newspaper*, September 2010.

Greenway Foundation. www.greenwayfoundation.org.

Hamaker, Gene E. *Irrigation Pioneers: A History of the Tri-County Project to 1935*. Minden NE: Warp, 1964.

Hoffman, Rocky. "Turkey Population at All-Time High," *NEBRASKAland*, March 2004, 46.

Johnsgard, Paul A. *Crane Music: A Natural History of American Cranes*. Lincoln: University of Nebraska Press, 1991.

Karl, Thomas R., Jerry M. Melillo, and Thomas C. Peterson, eds. *Global Climate Change Impacts in the United States*. New York: Cambridge University Press, 2009.

Kilgore, William H. *The Kilgore Journal of an Overland Journey to California in the Year 1850*. Edited by Joyce Rockwood Muench. New York: Hasting, 1949.

Klataske, Ron. Interview by the author, June 24, 2012.

Leopold, Aldo. *A Sand County Almanac and Sketches Here and There.* New York: Oxford University Press, 1968.

Leopold, Luna B., M. Gordon Wolman, and John P. Miller. *Fluvial Processes in Geomorphology.* New York: Dover, 1992.

Lingle, Gary. Interview by the author, May 4, 2010.

Mattes, Merrill J. *The Great Platte River Road: The Covered Wagon Mainline via Fort Kearny to Fort Laramie.* Lincoln: Nebraska State Historical Society, 1969.

Melville, Herman. *Moby Dick.* New York: Signet, 1961.

"Mid-State: For Decades It's Been a Plan." *Grand Island Independent*, July 19, 1975, 1-B.

Nebraska Environmental Trust. *2005 Annual Report to Nebraska Citizens.* Lincoln: Nebraska Environmental Trust, 2005.

Northern Colorado Water Conservancy District. "Colorado–Big Thompson Project." Northern Water. www.northernwater.org/Water Projects/C-BTProject.aspx.

———. "Colorado–Big Thompson Project Map." Northern Water. www. northernwater.org/docs/Water_Projects/PDFmapsWaterProjs/CBT Map2.pdf.

Northern Prairie Wildlife Research Center. *The Platte River Ecology Study: Special Research Report.* USGS Northern Prairie Wildlife Research Center Paper 248. Jamestown ND: U.S. Fish and Wildlife Service, 1981.

"$157M for Platte Gets Bush OK." *Kearney Hub*, May 9, 2008.

Parkman, Francis. *The Oregon Trail.* Edited by E. N. Feltskog. Lincoln: University of Nebraska Press, 1994.

Parks, Douglas R., and Waldo R. Wedel. "Pawnee Geography: Historical and Sacred." *Great Plains Quarterly* 5 (1985): 143–76.

Platte River Recovery Implementation Program. Program document. October 24, 2006. https://www.platteriverprogram.org/PubsAndData /Pages/ProgramLibrary.aspx.

Reisner, Marc. *Cadillac Desert: The American West and Its Disappearing Water.* Rev. ed. New York: Penguin, 1993.

Shoemaker, Thomas G. "Wildlife and Water Projects on the Platte River." In *Audubon Wildlife Report, 1988/1989,* edited by William

J. Chandler, 285–334. New York: National Audubon Society/Academic Press, 1988.

Stevenson, Robert Louis. *From Scotland to Silverado*. Edited by James D. Hart. Cambridge MA: Belknap, 1966.

Thorsen, Sam. "Wildlife Sanctuary Set near Gibbon." *Lincoln (NE) Sunday Journal and Star*, April 1, 1973.

U.S. Department of the Interior, Bureau of Reclamation. "Bureau of Reclamation — Dams." Last modified January 24, 2008. www.usbr.gov /projects/dams.jsp.

——— . *The Platte River Channel: History and Restoration*. Bureau of Reclamation Technical Service Center: Denver, 2004.

U.S. Department of the Interior, Bureau of Reclamation and U.S. Fish and Wildlife Service. *Platte River Recovery Implementation Program: Final Environmental Impact Statement*. Vol. 1. Casper WY: Bureau of Reclamation and U.S. Fish and Wildlife Service, 2006.

U.S. Fish and Wildlife Service. *Whooping Crane Recovery Plan*. Albuquerque NM: U.S. Fish and Wildlife Service, 1994.

Weltfish, Gene. *The Lost Universe: Pawnee Life and Culture*. Lincoln: University of Nebraska Press, 1977.

Yoder, Bruce. "Audubon Society Opposes Mid-State." *Kearney Hub*, August 16, 1973, 1.

——— . "Mid-State Claims Disputed." *Kearney Hub*, August 30, 1973, 1.

——— . "Mid-State Foes Gather." *Kearney Hub*, September 4, 1975, 1.